The Medieval Cookbook:

Old Cookbook Secrets & Tasting Medieval Recipes Revived for Modern Kitchens

Lily Heritage

Unlock Your Exclusive Free Bonus!

Thank you for choosing my book:

The Medieval Cookbook: Old Cookbook Secrets & Tasting Medieval Recipes Revived for Modern Kitchens

As a token of my gratitude, I've prepared a special gift for you:

an exclusive bonus book, absolutely FREE!

To claim your gift, just send me an email at **mosaicmediapublishing@gmail.com**

with the subject *Medieval Cookbook* ".

I'm thrilled to share this additional content with you and hope you'll love it as much as I do!

Table of Contents

Introduction

Preface

This book has been meticulously crafted to transport you into the historical tapestry of medieval cuisine, reinterpreted with a modern twist. At the heart of this endeavor is a commitment to preserving and valorizing a pivotal aspect of our gastronomic heritage, making it both accessible and enjoyable to contemporary audiences. Medieval cuisine transcends being merely a collection of ancient recipes; it serves as a profound medium to explore the everyday life, cultural traditions, and societal norms of those times. Through the culinary lens, we can gain insights into the societal stratification from the opulent banquets of the nobility to the modest meals of the peasantry.

As you delve into the pages of this book, you will uncover the culinary practices of the Middle Ages, learning about the ingredients and techniques that were staples of that era. You will appreciate the importance of spices, once considered rare luxuries, and observe how meals varied significantly across different social strata, adapting to the resources that were available. The book also illuminates how culinary habits were closely linked to religious observances and the rhythm of the seasons, illustrating the ingenuity of medieval cooks who thrived despite the absence of modern conveniences like refrigerators or contemporary kitchen technologies.

Moreover, this book guides you on how to bring these age-old recipes into the present day, employing modern ingredients and cooking methods. It's not just about replicating historical dishes but reimagining them in ways that resonate with today's gastronomic preferences. The aim is to breathe new life into historical culinary practices while encouraging creativity and enjoyment in modern cooking. You will discover useful tips for substituting elusive ingredients and creative ideas for presenting these dishes in an enticing contemporary format.

For anyone passionate about history, cooking, or simply exploring new culinary landscapes, this book offers a unique journey through time, where historical flavors meet modern palates. Prepare to embark on a culinary adventure that revives forgotten recipes, introduces you to novel tastes, and brings a slice of history right to your dining table. With its rich flavors and unique ingredient combinations, medieval cuisine can provide a sumptuously rich and fulfilling experience, infusing our everyday lives with a dash of historical enchantment.

Introduction to Reinterpreted Medieval Cuisine

History and Context of Medieval Cuisine

Medieval cuisine offers a captivating journey back in time, filled with culinary traditions that provide deep insights into the society of that era. Spanning from around 500 to 1500 AD, cooking styles varied significantly across regions, seasons, and available ingredients. Medieval cooking was not merely about sustenance; it also reflected one's social class, religious beliefs, and wealth level. The stark differences in social classes heavily influenced the ingredients used, cooking techniques, and how meals were consumed.

Nobles had access to exotic and expensive ingredients like spices from the East, while peasants settled for a simpler diet comprising grains, legumes, and seasonal vegetables. Sought-after spices such as black pepper, saffron, cinnamon, and cloves were not just used for flavoring but also symbolized wealth and power, often featured in noble banquets to display the host's prestige. In contrast, peasants utilized locally available herbs like sage, thyme, and parsley to enhance their dishes, which were easier to grow and essential for making food tastier.

Medieval cooking techniques were limited by the tools available, such as clay pots, roasting grids, and rudimentary ovens. These tools shaped how food was prepared, and cooks had to adapt to long cooking times and less precise temperature control. Most dishes were cooked over open fires using clay or metal pots. Preservation techniques like salting, drying, and smoking were crucial for keeping food available year-round, especially during the winter months. These methods allowed food to be stored for extended periods, ensuring survival during the hardest times. Dishes often featured a mix of sweet and savory flavors, with a liberal use of honey to sweeten both sweet and savory preparations, typical of medieval banquets and a unique characteristic of the era's cuisine.

Religion also profoundly influenced dietary habits. Events like Lent and religious festivals dictated the types of dishes prepared. For example, during Lent, meat was forbidden, and meals consisted of fish, legumes, and vegetables, while festive dishes were richer and often meat-based, seasoned with fine spices. These lean days led to the creation of many creative recipes using simple ingredients to prepare tasty and nutritious dishes. During Lent, dishes often included freshwater fish like trout or eel, and almond milk was used as a dairy substitute. The need to adhere to these dietary restrictions pushed cooks to develop ingenious recipes, creatively utilizing available resources.

Noble banquets were extravagant affairs where dishes were elaborately decorated and accompanied by music and performances. For instance, peacocks were often cooked and then adorned with their feathers to impress guests, and sugar centerpieces were used to decorate tables. These banquets were displays of power and prestige, with every detail crafted to awe guests. Conversely, peasant meals were much simpler and usually consumed within the family. Bread was a staple for all social classes, but its quality varied: nobles ate white, refined bread, while peasants had darker, denser bread made from whole grains or mixed cereals. Bread too reflected social status and was considered an essential part of the daily diet.

The variety of medieval recipes also depended on the seasons and the availability of ingredients. In summer, more fresh vegetables, fruits, and aromatic herbs were available, while in winter, preserved foods like dried legumes, smoked meats, and salted fish were used. This seasonality was fundamental to medieval cuisine and required cooks to constantly adapt to the available resources. Thus, the kitchen was highly flexible and creative, with each dish varying according to the time of year.

Reinterpreting Medieval Recipes with Modern Ingredients and Techniques

Adapting medieval recipes to modern tastes and habits requires a delicate balance between historical authenticity and practicality. Many medieval ingredients are either hard to find today or no longer play a significant role in our cooking. However, thanks to modern cooking techniques and the availability of numerous ingredients, we can reinterpret these dishes while preserving their original character.

Spice Adaptation: In medieval times, spices were a symbol of wealth and were used liberally, but today we can use them more judiciously to suit modern palates. For example, long pepper and mace, which are hard to find, can be replaced with black pepper and nutmeg to maintain a similar flavor profile. Additionally, using fresh aromatic herbs such as rosemary and thyme can add depth to dishes without making them overly spicy.

Cooking Techniques: Methods like open fire cooking can be reimagined using modern grills or ovens, achieving similar results with less difficulty. Sous-vide cooking is a fascinating alternative for recreating the slow cooking processes typical of medieval dishes, preserving the flavors and juiciness of the ingredients. This technique allows for tender and flavorful meats similar to those prepared in medieval kitchens but with greater control over the outcome.

Ingredient Substitution: Almond milk, commonly used in the Middle Ages, especially during fasting periods, can now be easily made at home or purchased ready-made. Game meat, which is difficult to source today, can be substituted with beef or chicken by adjusting cooking times and spices to achieve an authentic flavor. Marinades with red wine and aromatic herbs can be used to impart a richer flavor to the meat, mimicking the taste of game.

Modernizing Dishes: Reinterpreting medieval recipes isn't just about swapping ingredients; it's also about adapting these dishes for modern life. For example, a medieval pottage can be updated using a mix of fresh legumes and mild spices, served as a gourmet soup with crusty bread. Legume soups or savory pies can be transformed into sophisticated starters or main courses for social gatherings. Medieval savory pies, often filled with meat, vegetables, and spices, can be revamped using puff pastry or shortcrust pastry, making them easier to prepare. Even medieval sweets, typically made with honey and dried fruits, can be adapted by reducing the sugar content and adding fresh fruit to create lighter desserts.

The goal is to keep medieval culinary traditions alive, making them accessible and enjoyable for today's tastes. Medieval cuisine has much to offer, with flavors and techniques that can enrich our daily cooking and bring a piece of history to our tables. It's essential to approach these recipes with creativity and curiosity, exploring new ways to integrate them into modern cooking and adapt them to our tastes and lifestyles.

Medieval Ingredients and Modern Substitutions

Herbs and Spices: Modern Equivalents

Herbs and spices were among the most intriguing ingredients in medieval cuisine, known for their robust flavors and unique aromas. For instance, cinnamon was frequently used to flavor roasts and stews, adding a warm, spicy note. In the Middle Ages, the use of spices was a symbol of wealth and power because many of them came from distant lands like India, the Middle East, and the Far East, making them quite expensive. Some of the most commonly used spices were saffron, cinnamon, and cloves, cherished for their distinctive fragrance and flavor. Let's explore how we can use these spices today to preserve the authentic character of medieval recipes:

- **Saffron**: Highly valued in medieval times, saffron was used to impart a golden color and delicate flavor to dishes. It remains expensive but is readily available today. Saffron can be used to flavor risottos, soups, and stews, adding a refined touch. Even in small amounts, its distinctive floral aroma brings a special element to dishes. Saffron is also excellent in desserts like creams and custards, providing an elegant and aromatic effect. It's particularly good for enhancing the flavors of seafood dishes, such as paella or bouillabaisse.

- **Cinnamon**: Extensively used in both sweet and savory medieval dishes to add warmth and spice, cinnamon is still widely used today, especially in desserts. It can also be used to recreate medieval dishes in combination with other spices like cloves and nutmeg. Cinnamon is perfect for creating aromatic mixes and can be used in hot beverages like mulled wine or spiced cider to evoke the warm flavors of the past. Additionally, it can flavor meat dishes such as lamb or chicken, giving them a unique taste reminiscent of medieval culinary traditions.

- **Cloves**: Valued for their strong flavor and intense aroma, cloves were commonly used in medieval times to flavor meats and sauces. Today, they can be used sparingly in broths, marinades, and meat dishes so as not to overpower other flavors. Cloves are also ideal for flavoring sweets and fruit preserves, retaining the authentic character of medieval recipes. They can be used in meat marinades to add a spicy and slightly sweet flavor typical of noble preparations from the period.

By incorporating these spices into modern cooking, we can maintain the traditional essence of medieval recipes while adapting them to contemporary tastes and culinary techniques.

Grains, Dairy, and Legumes: Modern Adaptations

Medieval cuisine heavily relied on grains, dairy, and legumes as staples for most people. Many of these ingredients remain in our diet today, though some have evolved over time. Here's how we can adapt these ingredients to fit modern recipes:

- **Spelt and Barley:** In medieval times, spelt and barley were commonly used grains, especially among peasants. Spelt was utilized for making soups and pottages. Today, spelt has regained popularity as a healthy and versatile ingredient, rich in fiber, vitamins, and minerals. It's excellent for salads, soups, and one-pot dishes. Barley is still used in soups but can also be used to make risotto-like dishes called "orzotto." Both grains retain a rustic flavor and are perfect for adding an authentic touch to modern recipes. Spelt is also great for making bread and rustic focaccias, adding a rich flavor and texture reminiscent of medieval breads, while barley can be used in cold salads with fresh vegetables for a light but flavorful summer dish.

- **Almond Milk and Modern Alternatives:** Almond milk was very common in medieval times, particularly during fasting periods when animal products were not consumed. It was traditionally made at home by grinding almonds and mixing them with water. Today, almond milk is readily available in stores and can be used as an alternative to cow's milk in many medieval recipes. Other modern options include oat milk or soy milk, which can provide a creamy texture to dishes, accommodating dietary needs like vegan or lactose-free diets. Coconut milk can also be used to add an exotic flavor while still keeping the historical inspiration. Cashew and rice milk are other alternatives that offer different textures and can be used to prepare desserts and creamy sauces, enriching medieval recipes with new contemporary variations.

These adaptations allow us to preserve the historical essence of medieval recipes while integrating them into the culinary practices of today, making them more accessible and suitable for modern diets and preferences.

Meat, Fish, and Vegetarian Alternatives

In the Middle Ages, meat was a luxury reserved for the nobility, while peasants consumed it only on special occasions. Fish, on the other hand, was much more common, especially on prescribed fasting days by the Church. Vegetarian alternatives were also widely used, especially in monasteries. Let's see how we can adapt these traditions to modern recipes.

- **Game Meat and Modern Meat Cuts:** Game such as deer, boar, and pheasant were highly valued in medieval courts. Today, these types of meat are less common, but we can substitute them with more readily available cuts of beef, pork, or chicken. For instance, beef can be marinated with herbs and wine to replicate the robust flavor of game, while chicken can be cooked with spices like juniper and rosemary to achieve a similar taste to game meats. Modern cooking techniques like sous-vide, which involves cooking food at a low temperature in vacuum-sealed bags, help achieve tender and juicy meats reminiscent of slow medieval cooking. Using a smoker can also add a rustic flavor reminiscent of dishes from that era. Additionally, for those who want to approach the flavors of game without sourcing specific meats, pork can be marinated with robust spices and cooked slowly to achieve a satisfying and similar taste.

- **Fish and Vegetarian Alternatives:** Fish was a significant part of the medieval diet, especially on fasting days. Freshwater fish like trout and eels were common and were often cooked with spices and herb-based sauces. Today, we can prepare fish with simple methods like steaming or en papillote (cooking in a folded pouch), using aromatic herbs to give a flavor similar to medieval times. Vegetarian alternatives, such as legume soups and vegetable pies, were popular in monasteries and can be reinterpreted today to create tasty and nutritious dishes. Legumes like lentils and chickpeas can be used to prepare soups, veggie burgers, or patties, maintaining the spirit of medieval recipes but adapting them to today's tastes. Additionally, savory pies filled with spinach, chard, and cheese can be made using modern pastries like puff pastry or shortcrust pastry, making these recipes more accessible and quicker to prepare. Legume soups can be enhanced with modern spices to add depth of flavor, while seasonal vegetables can be grilled or roasted to create simple but tasty side dishes that recall medieval flavors.

In conclusion, reinterpreting medieval cuisine means finding a balance between authenticity and innovation. We can maintain the spirit of the original recipes while adapting them to modern tastes and needs. For example, a dish like medieval pottage can be revisited with fresh ingredients and lighter spices, served as a rustic but refined soup. Spices, grains, meat, and vegetarian alternatives offer many possibilities to rediscover the flavors of the past and bring them to our tables in a new way. This allows us to appreciate the richness of medieval cuisine and make it interesting and suitable for today's life. Another example could be a savory pie made with seasonal vegetables and goat cheese, baked until it has a golden and crispy crust: a combination that merges the authentic taste of the past with a modern twist, perfect for a special lunch or dinner.

Medieval Cooking Techniques Adapted for Today

From Open Fire to Modern Oven

In medieval times, cooking over an open fire was the primary method for preparing food. This technique was used for both meat and vegetables and required careful attention to control the fire and temperature. Foods were often cooked on spits, grills, or in terracotta pots placed over the fire.

Spit Cooking: Spit roasting was very common for cooking meats, especially during large feasts and banquets where entire animals such as pigs, deer, or birds were cooked. This method was not only about food preparation but also a display of skill, as it was crucial to know how to turn and cook the meat to keep it juicy and flavorful.

Today, we can adapt these ancient techniques using modern tools such as barbecues or ovens. For instance, spit-roasted meat can be prepared using a barbecue, which allows for even cooking and a smoky flavor reminiscent of the medieval open fire. With the barbecue, we can also use different types of wood or charcoal, such as oak, cherry, or hickory, adding unique aromas to the meat. Each type of wood imparts a distinct flavor: oak gives a robust aroma, while cherry adds a sweet and fruity touch. Moreover, for slow cooking like that needed for pork or beef, we can use a low-temperature oven to achieve tender and juicy meat, similar to the long cooking times over the fire. The barbecue also allows us to use spices and marinades that caramelize during cooking, creating a flavorful and delicious crust.

Terracotta Pot Cooking: Another medieval technique was cooking in terracotta pots, which were placed directly among the coals. This method imparted a smoky flavor to the food and allowed for slow and even cooking. Today, we can use cast iron or ceramic pots to replicate this type of cooking. Cast iron pots, in particular, retain heat well and are perfect for stews and soups, helping to recreate the ambiance of ancient medieval kitchens. An example of a dish that suits cast iron cooking well is vegetable pottage, a thick stew of vegetables, legumes, and spices that, when cooked slowly, develops rich flavors and a creamy texture, much like medieval preparations. Additionally, cast iron pots can also be used in the oven, making them ideal for long cookings that require even heat distribution.

Refractory Stone Cooking: A modern technique that recalls medieval cooking is the use of refractory stones. These stones, heated in the oven, are ideal for baking bread and focaccias as done in the wood-fired ovens of the Middle Ages. This gives the bread an authentic flavor and a crispy crust reminiscent of traditional preparations. Stone cooking is particularly useful for pizzas and focaccias, as it provides intense and direct heat that replicates a wood-fired oven.

Preservation Techniques: From Salting to Refrigerated Storage

In the Middle Ages, preserving food was crucial, especially during winter when fresh food was scarce. Key preservation techniques included salting, drying, and smoking. Salting was used to preserve meat and fish as salt removed moisture and inhibited bacterial growth. Smoking not only preserved food but also imparted a unique flavor and helped it last longer. These techniques required skill, as a mistake in salting could render food unsafe to eat.

Today, these traditional methods can be adapted using modern techniques. For example, salting is not only used for preservation but also to enhance flavor. Brining is popular for marinating meat and fish, making them tender and flavorful. Smoking has become much easier with home smokers, which allow achieving the typical smoky flavor even without a large outdoor space. We can also use flavored wood chips, such as cherry or apple, to add unique flavors during the smoking process. Drying has been modernized with the use of electric dehydrators, enabling the practical and safe preparation of dried meats (jerky) or dried fruits, keeping the tradition alive.

Refrigerated storage has changed how we keep food fresh, but some medieval techniques are still useful for adding flavor. Fermentation, for example, was used to preserve vegetables and dairy products and is being rediscovered not only for its preservative capabilities but also for its health benefits. Preparations like sauerkraut or kefir were present in the Middle Ages and can be easily made at home today, maintaining an ancient tradition that aligns well with modern healthy eating trends. Fermentation not only extends food's shelf life but also enriches it with complex flavors and health benefits for the gut.

Another medieval preservation technique we can adapt today is fat preservation, used for preserving cooked meats like duck confit. Today, this technique can be used to add depth of flavor to meats and, with the addition of modern spices, achieve even more sophisticated results. Moreover, we can use olive oil instead of animal fat to preserve vegetables, mushrooms, or cheeses, creating preparations that combine tradition and modernity.

Pairing and Balancing Flavors in Modern Recipes

Medieval cuisine was celebrated for its generous use of spices and the remarkable balance it achieved between sweet and savory flavors. Dishes often incorporated meat with dried fruits, honey, or sugar, resulting in a contrast of flavors that might seem unusual today but were greatly appreciated in their time. This intriguing balance of flavors can be effectively reintroduced in contemporary recipes, adjusted to suit modern palates. The fusion of sweet and savory, a hallmark of noble medieval kitchens, allows us to rediscover complex and fascinating flavors.

Sweet and Sour Sauce Pairings: One medieval combination we can reinterpret today involves the use of sweet and sour sauces to accompany meats. In the Middle Ages, these sauces typically combined vinegar, honey, and a mix of spices, striking a perfect balance between acidity and sweetness. Modern cooks can recreate these flavors using balsamic vinegar and brown sugar, enhanced with spices such as cinnamon and ginger, to accompany roasts or grilled meats, thus bringing medieval culinary traditions to life. Balsamic vinegar offers a more nuanced sweetness compared to the simpler wine vinegar of the past, while brown sugar serves as a more accessible substitute for the raw, expensive sugars once used. These contemporary ingredients maintain the essential balance between sweet and sour, are readily available, and enhance the flavor profile of dishes. Additionally, incorporating fresh fruits like cherries or blueberries can introduce further complexity and a refreshing element that balances the robust flavors of the meat.

Meat and Fruit Combinations: The pairing of meat with fruit was commonplace at medieval banquets. Meats such as duck or pork were often served with plums, raisins, or apples to create a delightful contrast. This approach can be adapted in today's kitchens by incorporating fresh or dried fruits into roasts or stews, adding an element of complexity to the dish and a subtle sweetness that complements the richness of the meat. Dried fruits like figs and dates are particularly effective for stuffing meats such as chicken or turkey, offering a delightful contrast between the savory meat and the fruit's natural sweetness. The use of citrus fruits like oranges or lemons can inject a welcome acidity that highlights the flavors of the spices and the meat, enriching the overall dining experience.

Utilizing Spices to Enhance Flavors: Spices were a fundamental component of medieval cuisine, used not only to season but also to signify wealth and status. Pepper, cinnamon, cloves, and mace were staples that added depth and complexity to meals, creating a rich and varied aromatic profile that was much prized. These spices, often sourced from distant lands, were a luxury that symbolized wealth and power. Today, we can employ these spices thoughtfully and innovatively in new recipes that honor the traditions of the past while catering to contemporary taste preferences. By moderating their use and experimenting with new combinations, these spices can transform a simple meal into an extraordinary culinary adventure that bridges the centuries.

Reimagined Recipes

Appetizers and Light Dishes

Introduction: Origins and Reinterpretation of Medieval Appetizers

Medieval appetizers and light dishes were crafted from simple, wholesome ingredients such as soups, herb-infused focaccias, barley and vegetable pottages, and other vegetable-based dishes, all utilizing the seasonal and local produce available. These dishes truly exemplified the essence of medieval cuisine: a cuisine that was straightforward yet bursting with flavor, where each ingredient was given a chance to shine. Individuals from the lower social strata often prepared starters with grains, legumes, and vegetables, predominantly grown in their own gardens or gathered from local fields and forests. Soups and pottages were staple dishes that not only ensured a healthy diet but also maximized the utilization of available resources in a sustainable, waste-free manner.

Fresh vegetables were plucked straight from the garden and often served as the primary source of nourishment for the poorer classes. In contrast, the upper classes enjoyed the luxury of incorporating meat and more expensive ingredients into their meals. Spices, expensive and difficult to acquire, were rarely featured in the appetizers of the less affluent. Luxury spices like pepper, cinnamon, and cloves were exclusive to the nobility, sourced from distant lands such as India and the Spice Islands, and were extremely challenging to obtain. As a result, the appetizers of the nobility could include more fragrant and sought-after ingredients. These starters were frequently embellished with exotic spices and honey to enrich the flavors and to impress guests at lavish banquets.

In contrast, in the homes of peasants, appetizers were simple and enhanced with local aromatic herbs like thyme, rosemary, and sage, which were cultivated in home gardens. These herbs were not only a cost-effective way to flavor food but were also used for their medicinal properties. They were incredibly versatile, used not only for enhancing taste but also for preserving food and treating minor health issues.

Typically, medieval appetizers were simple dishes that prepped the palate for the more hearty and substantial main courses to follow. At the tables of the nobility, however, appetizers could be quite elaborate and were served in small portions to not only impress guests but also to display the wealth and status of the host. Often, these dishes were adorned with edible flowers or vine leaves, adding an aesthetic element that echoed the grandeur of the feasts. These decorative touches were not merely for show; they carried symbolic meaning, representing a connection with nature and the changing seasons—concepts that were deeply ingrained in medieval culture.

The recipes in this section offer a modern take on these traditional dishes, aiming to preserve the rustic spirit of medieval cuisine while adapting it to contemporary taste preferences and nutritional needs. The modern iterations of these appetizers are lighter yet packed with flavors that hark back to bygone days. We utilize ingredients that are easily accessible today and employ cooking techniques that accentuate the natural flavors, maintaining the simplicity that was characteristic of the original preparations. These modernized appetizers are ideal for an engaging aperitif or as light starters for any meal, providing a blend of historical reverence and modern culinary innovation. We continue to incorporate fresh aromatic herbs and now more affordable spices, ensuring each dish remains distinctive. Additionally, the updated versions of these appetizers often feature ingredients that were not available in the medieval period, such as exotic vegetables and novel spices, and employ advanced cooking techniques, adding new layers of flavor and texture to each dish. These enhancements allow us to reimagine medieval cuisine in a way that resonates with today's gourmet expectations while paying homage to its historical roots.

Reinterpreting Cooking Techniques

A hallmark of medieval culinary practices was the reliance on basic, yet effective cooking methods such as open-fire cooking and the use of wood-fired ovens. These traditional methods imparted a distinctively rustic and smoky flavor to the dishes that we can replicate today using modern equipment like barbecues or home ovens. Focaccias, for example, were traditionally baked directly on the stones of wood-fired ovens, gaining a crispy texture and a subtly smoky taste. Today, a baking stone in a home oven can produce similar results, providing even cooking and a crispy crust that mimics the textures of medieval breadmaking. Utilizing a convection oven or a baking stone not only maintains the authentic flavor profile but simplifies the cooking process. The baking stone, in particular, effectively distributes heat, simulating the conditions of ancient wood-fired ovens and eliminating the need for continuous fire adjustment.

Soups were a staple in medieval cuisine, commonly prepared with a mix of cereals, legumes, and whatever vegetables were in season. These soups often incorporated stale bread, which was used to thicken the mixture and enhance its texture, resulting in a heartier, creamier dish. Modern cooks can achieve a similar thickening effect using croutons or finely ground breadcrumbs. Additionally, reinterpreting these traditional soups with contemporary ingredients such as rich, homemade broths, can elevate the depth of flavor. Adding fresh aromatic herbs and a drizzle of olive oil can infuse freshness and enhance the flavor complexity, aligning with modern culinary preferences which favor nuanced and layered taste profiles. Introducing elements like a dash of fresh lemon juice or a splash of balsamic vinegar can also balance the richness of the soups with a touch of acidity, making them more appealing to today's palate.

Vegetables played a significant role in medieval diets, often appearing in dishes like salads and savory pies. Traditionally, these vegetables were boiled or steamed and dressed simply with vinegar and oil. Modern cooking techniques allow for more diverse preparations: grilling vegetables brings out their natural sugars and adds a smoky flavor, while sous-vide cooking locks in nutrients and flavors, achieving perfectly tender yet crisp textures. In the realm of savory pies, utilizing lighter, flakier pastries such as puff or shortcrust pastry transforms these dishes into more delicate and appealing offerings compared to their heavier medieval counterparts. The sous-vide technique, in particular, offers a contemporary twist to vegetable cooking, allowing for precise temperature control that ensures vegetables are cooked just right – tender but with intact flavors and nutrients, closely mirroring the quality and freshness that medieval cooks aimed for, but with a modern, lighter touch. This method not only honors the traditional practices but also adapts them to suit modern-day health and dietary preferences, making ancient recipes accessible and enjoyable in the contemporary culinary landscape.

Flavor Pairings and Contrasts

In the Middle Ages, the interplay of sweet and salty flavors was highly valued, often showcasing dishes that combined dried fruits such as figs and raisins with savory ingredients like cheeses or meats. A contemporary version of this pairing might be focaccia topped with figs and goat cheese, which harmonizes the sweetness of the fruit with the saltiness of the cheese, creating a delightful contrast. This type of pairing can be subtly reintroduced today, using fresh or dried fruit in modest amounts to balance flavors and add a sweet note without overwhelming the dish. For example, a rosemary focaccia could be enhanced with a few grapes to introduce a flavor contrast, or a savory pie might include a filling of ricotta and figs to evoke typical medieval tastes. Additionally, playing with other contrasts, such as drizzling honey over aged cheese, can add a balanced sweetness that enriches the dish without making it overly heavy.

These modern combinations, while maintaining medieval traditions, are designed to suit contemporary tastes, offering intriguing and well-balanced dishes that blend tradition and innovation. The reinterpretation of medieval appetizers presented in this section aims to combine the authenticity of traditional recipes with the practicality and lightness of modern cuisine. We have preserved the focus on seasonality and ingredient availability, as was common in medieval times, and reintroduced the rustic flavors that characterized the appetizers of that era. At the same time, we have enhanced these recipes with modern touches to make them more appealing and suitable for today's palates. These appetizers are designed to be shared, recreating the sense of conviviality typical of medieval tables and offering a taste of history that can surprise and delight today's guests. With these dishes, we hope to revive the flavors of the past, making them accessible and enjoyable for anyone who wishes to rediscover medieval cuisine with a contemporary twist.

Barley and Root Vegetable Soup

This hearty soup has its origins in the rural regions of Central Europe, particularly in areas of modern-day Germany, Austria, and Poland, where it was traditionally prepared as a warm and nourishing dish during harsh winters. Its simplicity and wholesome flavor have helped it spread across many European regions, and it is still appreciated today for its versatility and comforting nature.

Preparation Time: 20 minutes

Total Time: 1 hour 15 minutes

Servings: 4

Ingredients:

- 1 cup pearl barley (approx. 200 ml or 190 grams of pearl barley)
- 2 medium carrots
- 1 parsnip
- 1 onion
- 2 cloves garlic
- 2 tablespoons extra virgin olive oil (approx. 30 ml)
- 4 cups vegetable broth (approx. 950 ml)
- 1 bay leaf
- 1 sprig fresh thyme
- Salt and pepper, to taste

- Fresh parsley for garnish
- Lemon zest (optional)
- 1 celery stalk
- 1 medium potato
- 1 teaspoon sweet paprika (approx. 5 ml)
- Toasted rustic bread, for serving

Instructions:

1. **Prepare the Ingredients:** Rinse the pearl barley under cold running water and drain well. This step helps to remove excess starch and impurities, ensuring a cleaner flavor, a clearer broth, and a better texture. Peel the carrots, parsnip, and potato, then cut them into approximately ½-inch cubes. Finely chop the onion, garlic, and celery stalk.

2. **Sauté:** In a large pot, heat the olive oil over medium heat (around 320-340°F), being careful not to overheat the oil to avoid burning the garlic. The oil should be hot but not smoking, and the garlic should start to sizzle gently when added. Add the chopped onion, garlic, and celery, and sauté for 5-7 minutes until they become soft and translucent. The celery adds complexity to the aromatic base, making the soup more flavorful.

3. **Cook the Vegetables:** Add the diced carrots, parsnip, and potato to the pot and cook for an additional 7-8 minutes, stirring occasionally to let the vegetables absorb the flavors. Add the paprika, which will give the soup a richer color and a slight smoky note.

4. **Add Barley and Broth:** Add the drained barley to the vegetables and mix well. Pour in the warm vegetable broth, add the bay leaf and thyme sprig, and bring to a boil. Reduce the heat, cover, and simmer. If you like a fresher note, you can add a bit of lemon zest just before serving to preserve its fragrance.

5. **Simmer:** Let the soup cook over low heat for about 45-50 minutes, or until the barley and vegetables are tender. Stir occasionally, and add more broth or hot water if needed to maintain the desired consistency. The goal is a creamy, well-blended soup where all the ingredients come together smoothly.

6. **Seasoning:** Remove the bay leaf and thyme sprig. Adjust the salt and pepper to taste. For a creamier consistency, lightly mash some of the vegetables with the back of a spoon, or use an immersion blender to partially blend the soup, leaving some vegetable pieces for a varied texture. This balance between creamy and chunky enhances both the visual appeal and mouthfeel.

7. **Serve:** Serve the soup hot, garnished with a sprinkle of chopped fresh parsley and a drizzle of extra virgin olive oil. You may also add grated Parmesan cheese or croutons for extra flavor

and texture. Serve with toasted rustic bread rubbed with a clove of garlic for an added layer of flavor and crunch.

8. **Variations and Tips**:

- **Customize the Soup:** You can adapt this soup to your taste and available ingredients. For an earthier, fall-inspired flavor, add some sliced fresh mushrooms during the sauté step. If you want a higher-protein version, add legumes such as chickpeas or beans in the last 15 minutes of cooking. For a richer, velvety soup, stir in some heavy cream at the end of cooking, or use coconut milk for a lactose-free or vegan version.

Swiss Chard and Ricotta Ravioli

Swiss Chard and Ricotta Ravioli is a traditional recipe rooted in the rural regions of central Italy, particularly Tuscany and Umbria. The combination of fresh greens and ricotta has been used for centuries to create flavorful and nutritious dishes. This recipe has remained popular through the ages, celebrated for its simplicity and the rich flavors that evoke the tastes of the past. Even today, Swiss Chard and Ricotta Ravioli is cherished as a special first course, perfect for festive occasions.

Prep Time: 45 minutes

Total Time: 1 hour 30 minutes

Servings: 4

Ingredients:

- 2 1/2 cups all-purpose flour (approx. 312.5 grams)
- 3 large eggs
- 10.5 oz Swiss chard (fresh) (approx. 300 grams)
- 9 oz ricotta cheese (approx. 255 grams)
- 1/2 cup grated Parmesan cheese (approx. 50 grams)
- 1 garlic clove
- 2 tbsp extra virgin olive oil (approx. 30 ml)
- Ground nutmeg, to taste
- Salt and pepper, to taste
- Butter and sage leaves for dressing

- Grated lemon zest (optional)
- 1 tbsp breadcrumbs (optional, approx. 15 grams)

Instructions:

1. **Prepare the Dough:** On a clean work surface, make a well in the flour and crack the eggs into the center. Beat the eggs with a fork, gradually incorporating the flour from the sides. Continue kneading with your hands for about 10-15 minutes, until you have a smooth and elastic dough. If the dough feels too stiff, add a tablespoon of warm water to soften it. Use the palms of your hands to push and fold the dough, developing the gluten for the best consistency. The dough should feel silky and non-sticky. If it is too sticky, add a bit more flour until it reaches the correct consistency. If it's too dry, add a teaspoon of warm water at a time until smooth and pliable. Wrap it in plastic wrap and let it rest for at least 30-45 minutes at room temperature. This resting period allows the gluten to relax, making the dough easier to roll out.

2. **Prepare the Filling:** Meanwhile, wash the Swiss chard thoroughly and boil it in salted water for about 5 minutes. Drain well and squeeze out any excess water, then chop it finely. In a skillet, heat the extra virgin olive oil and sauté the crushed garlic clove for 2-3 minutes, until golden. Add the chopped chard and cook for a few minutes, stirring frequently. Remove the garlic and let the chard cool to avoid melting the ricotta when assembling the filling.

3. **Mix the Filling:** In a mixing bowl, combine the cooled Swiss chard, ricotta cheese, grated Parmesan, a pinch of nutmeg, salt, and pepper. If the filling seems too wet, add a tablespoon of breadcrumbs to absorb the excess moisture. Before proceeding, check the consistency of the filling to ensure it's not too liquid, which could cause the ravioli to burst during cooking. Mix thoroughly until smooth and creamy. For added freshness, you can add some grated lemon zest to the filling.

4. **Roll Out the Dough:** Using a rolling pin or a pasta machine, roll the dough into a thin sheet about 1-2 mm thick. Make sure the dough is as uniform as possible to ensure even cooking. Place small mounds of filling on the sheet, spacing them a few centimeters apart. Cover with another sheet of pasta and press down around the filling to seal the ravioli, making sure to remove any air pockets to prevent them from bursting during cooking. Use a pasta cutter to cut out the ravioli and make sure they are sealed well. For extra security, press the edges with a fork to avoid opening during cooking.

5. **Cook the Ravioli:** Bring a large pot of salted water to a boil. Cook the ravioli for 3-4 minutes or until they float to the surface. Carefully remove them with a slotted spoon to avoid breaking them. Avoid overcrowding the pot to prevent the ravioli from sticking together.

6. **Prepare the Sauce:** In a skillet, melt the butter over medium heat with a few fresh sage leaves. Let the sage infuse the butter for 2-3 minutes until it becomes slightly nutty. Add the drained ravioli and sauté them gently for a minute, ensuring they are well coated with the sage butter. You can add a pinch of coarse salt to enhance the flavors.

7. **Serve:** Serve the ravioli hot, arranging them on plates and topping them with a sprinkle of grated Parmesan cheese. For a final touch, drizzle with a little extra virgin olive oil and add a few crispy sage leaves for decoration. These ravioli make an ideal first course for a special dinner, bringing back the authentic taste of traditional Italian cuisine. Pair with a glass of Pinot Grigio or Vermentino to complete the experience.

8. **Variations and Tips:**

   - **Alternative Cheese:** Substitute the ricotta with sheep's milk cheese for a milder flavor, or use blue cheese for a more intense, distinct taste.
   - **Texture Addition:** Add finely chopped walnuts to the filling for extra crunch and flavor.
   - **Sauce Alternative:** You can also serve the ravioli with a lightly spiced tomato sauce for a rustic and bold variation.
   - **Make-Ahead Tip:** These ravioli can be made in advance and frozen: lay them on a floured tray, freeze, and then transfer them to a food-safe bag. This way, you'll always have a delicious dish ready for any special occasion.

Medieval Onion Tart

The onion tart is a recipe that dates back to medieval times, originating in the regions of Central Europe, particularly in Alsace and Bavaria. Simple ingredients like onions and eggs were commonly used to create hearty, nutritious dishes. Over time, this recipe spread to other parts of Europe, becoming a beloved dish known for its rich flavor and versatility. Today, the onion tart remains a popular choice, especially in rustic versions that evoke its ancient roots.

Prep Time: 30 minutes

Total Time: 1 hour and 30 minutes

Servings: 6

Ingredients:

- pounds white onions (approximately 500 g)
- 1 rolled pie crust (or a 9-inch premade pie crust)
- tablespoons extra virgin olive oil
- tablespoons butter
- eggs
- 2/3 cup heavy cream (approximately 150 ml)
- 3.5 ounces grated cheese (preferably Gruyère or another hard cheese)
- 1 teaspoon fresh thyme, chopped
- Salt and pepper to taste
- A pinch of nutmeg

- 1 tablespoon honey (optional)
- 1 teaspoon Dijon mustard (optional)
- A few sprigs of rosemary for garnish

Instructions

1. **Prepare the Onions**: Peel the onions and slice them thinly, keeping the slices uniform for even cooking and an attractive presentation. White onions are ideal for this recipe due to their natural sweetness, which imparts a delicate but assertive flavor to the tart.

2. **Cook the Onions:** In a large skillet, heat the olive oil and butter over medium heat. Add the sliced onions and cook slowly for about 20-25 minutes, stirring occasionally. The onions should become soft and caramelized, taking on a deep golden color. This slow caramelization enhances the onions' natural sweetness, adding depth of flavor to the tart and creating a perfect contrast with the other ingredients. If you prefer a sweeter note, add a tablespoon of honey during the last few minutes of cooking. For best results, take your time with this step—the flavor of the tart depends on the perfectly caramelized onions.

3. **Prepare the Crust:** Preheat the oven to 350°F (180°C). Roll out the pie crust and place it in a 9-inch pie dish, pressing the crust into the edges. If you don't have a 9-inch pie dish, you can use a slightly larger or smaller one, adjusting the filling accordingly. Prick the bottom of the crust with a fork to prevent it from puffing up during baking. For a crisper base, blind bake the crust for about 10 minutes: cover it with parchment paper and fill it with pie weights or dried beans to keep it flat. This ensures the base will stay crispy when the filling is added.

4. **Prepare the Filling:** In a large bowl, whisk together the eggs and heavy cream until smooth and creamy. Add the grated cheese, chopped thyme, a generous pinch of nutmeg, salt, and pepper. For added flavor, mix in a teaspoon of Dijon mustard before adding the other ingredients—this will bring a slight kick that contrasts nicely with the onions. Mix well to ensure all ingredients are well incorporated.

5. **Assemble the Tart:** Spread the caramelized onions evenly over the pie crust, ensuring they cover the entire bottom. Pour the egg and cream mixture over the onions, leveling the surface with a spatula. Garnish with a few sprigs of rosemary for additional aroma and presentation.

6. **Bake:** Bake the tart in the preheated oven for 35-40 minutes, or until the surface is golden brown and the filling is set. Test for doneness by inserting a toothpick into the center—if it comes out clean, the tart is ready. If the surface starts browning too quickly, cover it with aluminum foil and continue baking.

7. **Serve:** Let the tart cool for at least 10 minutes before serving, allowing the filling to set and making it easier to slice. The onion tart can be enjoyed warm or at room temperature, and it makes an excellent appetizer or light dish. Serve it alongside a green salad dressed with

vinaigrette for a complete and balanced meal. For added crunch, consider tossing a few walnuts into the salad to complement the tart's flavors.

8. **Variations and Tips**

- **Additional Herbs:** Add fresh herbs like marjoram or parsley to vary the aromatic profile of the filling.
- **Different Cheeses:** Swap Gruyère for Pecorino or aged Parmesan if you prefer a more intense flavor. Pecorino offers a salty, bold taste, while Parmesan provides a complex and savory note.
- **Rustic Twist:** For a more rustic version, use whole wheat flour to make the pie crust, giving the tart a richer flavor and crunchier texture.
- **Enhance with Bacon:** Add a few slices of smoked bacon with the onions for extra richness, particularly appreciated in heartier versions of this medieval recipe.

Herb Focaccia

This herb focaccia has ancient origins, dating back to medieval times when it was prepared in Mediterranean regions, particularly Italy, using simple and readily available ingredients like flour, yeast, and aromatic herbs. It was especially popular in Liguria, where it was baked in communal village ovens and often used as a staple food during agricultural work due to its simplicity and portability. Focaccia remains a versatile and beloved dish, perfect for accompanying other foods or enjoyed on its own.

Preparation Time: 20 minutes (+ 1 hour and 30 minutes rising time)

Total Time: 2 hours and 10 minutes

Servings: 6-8

Ingredients:

- 4 cups all-purpose flour (approx. 500 grams)
- 1 1/4 cups warm water (approx. 300 ml)
- 2 1/4 teaspoons active dry yeast (or 0.7 oz fresh yeast) (approx. 7 grams dry yeast or 20 grams fresh yeast)
- 2 teaspoons salt (approx. 10 grams)
- 1 teaspoon sugar (approx. 4 grams)
- 1/4 cup extra virgin olive oil + extra for brushing (approx. 60 ml)
- 1 teaspoon fresh rosemary, chopped
- 1 teaspoon fresh thyme, chopped

- 1 teaspoon dried oregano
- Coarse salt for sprinkling

Instructions:

1. **Prepare the Dough**: In a large bowl, dissolve the active dry yeast in warm water along with the sugar. Let it sit for 5-10 minutes until a light foam forms on the surface, indicating that the yeast is activated and the dough will rise properly. In another bowl, mix the flour and salt, ensuring that the salt does not come into direct contact with the yeast initially.

2. **Mix and First Rise:** Pour the yeast mixture into the flour bowl and add the olive oil. Start mixing by hand or using a stand mixer with a dough hook. Knead for about 10 minutes until a soft, elastic dough forms. If the dough feels too sticky, add a little flour; if it feels too dry, add a tablespoon of water at a time. Achieving the correct consistency is crucial for a focaccia with the perfect softness and structure. Form the dough into a ball, place it in a lightly oiled bowl, cover with a damp cloth or plastic wrap, and let it rise in a warm place for about 1 hour or until doubled in size.

3. **Shape and Second Rise:** Once the dough has risen, transfer it to a lightly floured surface and stretch it gently by hand until it is about 3/4 inch thick. Place the dough on a baking sheet lined with parchment paper and let it rest for another 30 minutes. During this time, the dough will continue to rise, making it even fluffier.

4. **Prepare the Focaccia:** Preheat your oven to 400°F (200°C). Use your fingers to make small dimples on the surface of the dough, pressing gently. The dimples allow the olive oil to penetrate the dough, enhancing flavor and contributing to a crispy crust. Generously brush the top with extra virgin olive oil, making sure it settles into the dimples. Sprinkle the rosemary, thyme, and oregano evenly over the top, followed by a scattering of coarse salt for added crunch and flavor.

5. **Bake:** Bake the focaccia in the preheated oven for about 20-25 minutes, or until the top is golden brown and the focaccia is fully cooked. It should have a crispy crust and a soft, fluffy interior. If you prefer a softer crust, cover the focaccia with aluminum foil during the last 10 minutes of baking.

6. **Serve:** Let the focaccia cool on a wire rack before cutting it into pieces. Herb focaccia can be enjoyed on its own, as a side for cheese and cured meats, or as a base for gourmet sandwiches. You can also serve it with a drizzle of extra virgin olive oil for added flavor. Alternatively, you can sprinkle freshly grated Parmesan cheese or a few extra flakes of coarse salt for extra flavor and texture.

7. **Variations and Tips**

   - **Herbs:** Customize your focaccia by adding other herbs such as sage or marjoram.

- **Toppings:** For a richer focaccia, add pitted black olives or halved cherry tomatoes to the top before baking. Another interesting variation is to add thin slices of potato, previously tossed in olive oil and salt, for a delicious potato focaccia.
- **Flavor Enhancers:** If you want a more pronounced flavor, add a teaspoon of garlic powder or dried onion flakes to the dough, which will give an extra depth of flavor.

Medieval Pea Soup

This simple yet hearty soup dates back to medieval times when it was prepared with humble, nutritious ingredients. It was widespread across Europe, especially in rural villages where peas were a staple in the diets of farming communities due to their abundance and nutritional value. Particularly popular in the regions of Germany and France, the soup was often enjoyed during the cold months as a source of warmth and energy. Today, this soup is reinterpreted in a modern way, while retaining its rustic and authentic character.

Prep Time: 15 minutes

Total Time: 35 minutes

Servings: 4

Ingredients:

- 1 lb fresh or frozen peas (approx. 450 grams)
- 1 medium onion
- 1 medium potato
- 2 tablespoons extra virgin olive oil (approx. 30 ml)
- 4 1/4 cups vegetable broth (approx. 1 liter)
- Salt and pepper, to taste
- 1/2 cup heavy cream (optional) (approx. 120 ml)
- Juice of half a lemon
- 1 teaspoon sugar (optional) (approx. 4 grams)

- Croutons for serving (optional)

Instructions:

1. **Prepare the Ingredients:** Peel and finely chop the onion. Peel the potato and cut it into 1/2-inch cubes. The potato will add a creamy texture to the soup, while the peas provide a unique sweetness.

2. **Sauté the Onion:** In a large pot, heat the extra virgin olive oil over medium heat. Add the chopped onion and sauté for about 5-7 minutes, until soft and translucent, stirring often to prevent burning. If desired, add a teaspoon of sugar to help caramelize the onion, intensifying its flavor and adding extra sweetness that complements the peas.

3. **Cook the Soup:** Add the cubed potato to the pot and cook for another 5 minutes, stirring occasionally. Pour in the hot vegetable broth and bring to a boil. Once boiling, reduce the heat and let it simmer for about 15 minutes, or until the potatoes are tender. Keep the pot partially covered to maintain the right moisture level, allowing for some evaporation while concentrating the flavors.

4. **Add the Peas:** Add the fresh or frozen peas to the broth and cook for another 5-7 minutes, or until the peas are tender. Peas cook quickly, so be careful not to overcook them to preserve their bright green color and fresh flavor. If using fresh peas, make sure they are young and tender for the best texture and sweetness.

5. **Blend the Soup:** Remove the pot from the heat. Using an immersion blender, blend the soup until smooth and creamy. For a more rustic texture, leave some of the peas whole. If the soup is too thick, add a little more broth or hot water to achieve the desired consistency.

6. **Season the Soup:** Adjust the seasoning with salt and pepper to taste. If you want a creamier soup, add the heavy cream and stir well to combine. The cream will make the soup more velvety and rich. Add the lemon juice near the end of cooking to balance the sweetness of the peas and provide a hint of freshness. The lemon not only balances the flavors but also enhances the soup's bright green color.

7. **Serve:** Serve the soup hot, drizzled with a bit of extra virgin olive oil to enhance the flavor of the ingredients. You can also add a sprinkle of freshly ground black pepper for extra taste. To make the dish more filling, add some croutons, preferably garlic- or rosemary-flavored. The croutons add a delightful crunch that contrasts with the creamy texture of the soup.

8. **Variations and Tips**

   - **Add Garlic:** For a more intense flavor, add a clove of minced garlic when sautéing the onion, which will provide a deeper, aromatic note to the soup.

- **Vegan Option**: To make a vegan version, omit the cream and substitute it with coconut milk or cashew cream. Coconut milk will add a slight sweetness and exotic flavor, while cashew cream will provide a neutral creamy texture.
- **Garlic-Flavored Croutons**: Another interesting variation is to add garlic-flavored croutons for extra crunch. If you prefer a bit of spice, add a pinch of red pepper flakes during cooking for a gentle heat.
- **Fresh Herbs**: For an additional layer of flavor, add fresh basil while blending for a more aromatic soup. To make the soup more nutritious, add cooked white beans, which will increase the protein content and make it more substantial.
- **Garnish Ideas**: Garnish each bowl with a swirl of cream (if using). For a bit of crunch, add toasted pumpkin seeds or sliced almonds. These elements not only add texture but also create an interesting contrast with the sweetness of the soup.

Lentil Soup with Cumin

This lentil soup has ancient origins and was popular in various cultures of the Middle East and the Mediterranean, particularly in countries like Syria, Lebanon, and Egypt, where it was often prepared as a nutritious and hearty family meal. During the medieval period, lentils were a staple food in the peasant diet due to their abundance and high nutritional value. This soup, enriched with cumin and coriander, reflects the culinary influences that spread along trade routes and through the Crusades, making it an aromatic and hearty dish ideal for cold days.

Preparation Time: 20 minutes

Total Time: 50 minutes

Servings: 4

Ingredients:

- 1 1/4 cups red lentils (250 g)
- 1 large onion
- 2 garlic cloves
- 2 medium carrots
- 2 tablespoons extra virgin olive oil
- 1 teaspoon ground cumin
- 1 teaspoon ground coriander
- 4 1/4 cups vegetable broth (1 liter)
- 1 bay leaf

- Salt and pepper, to taste
- Juice of half a lemon
- Fresh chopped parsley, for garnish
- Croutons, for serving (optional)

Instructions:

1. **Prepare the Ingredients:** Rinse the lentils under cold running water until the water runs clear. Peel and finely chop the onion and garlic. Peel the carrots and cut them into 1 cm cubes. This initial preparation helps organize all the ingredients and simplifies the cooking process.

2. **Sauté the Vegetables:** In a large pot, heat the olive oil over medium heat. Add the chopped onion and sauté for about 5-7 minutes until soft and golden. Add the chopped garlic and cook for another minute until fragrant. This step develops a rich and aromatic base for the soup.

3. **Cook the Carrots and Spices:** Add the carrot cubes to the pot and cook for another 5 minutes, stirring occasionally. Add the ground cumin and coriander, and mix well to lightly toast the spices, releasing their aroma and enhancing the flavor. Toasting the spices allows their essential oils to be released, enriching the aromatic profile of the soup.

4. **Add Lentils and Broth:** Add the rinsed lentils to the pot and stir to coat them with the sautéed vegetables and spices. Pour in the hot vegetable broth and add the bay leaf. Bring to a boil, then reduce the heat and cover the pot. Let it simmer for about 25-30 minutes, or until the lentils are tender and creamy. Keep the pot partially covered to help maintain the right moisture level and allow slight evaporation, which helps concentrate the flavors. Stir occasionally and add more broth or hot water if needed to maintain the desired consistency.

5. **Seasoning:** Once the lentils are well cooked and the soup has reached a creamy consistency, remove the bay leaf. Adjust the salt and pepper to taste. Add the lemon juice at the end of cooking to preserve its freshness and acidity, balancing the flavors and enhancing the overall taste.

6. **Blend (Optional):** If you prefer a smoother soup, blend a portion with an immersion blender, leaving some chunks for added texture. Alternatively, you can skip this step for a more rustic consistency.

7. **Serve:** Serve the soup hot, garnished with a sprinkle of fresh chopped parsley and a drizzle of extra virgin olive oil. If desired, accompany with croutons for added crunch. You can rub the croutons with garlic for extra flavor. This soup is perfect as a main dish or a hearty appetizer, ideal for cold evenings with its rich and spiced flavor.

8. **Presentation:** Presentation is key to making the soup inviting. Garnish each bowl with some fresh parsley and a lemon wedge for added color. For more flavor, sprinkle some toasted

cumin seeds over the soup, adding both a crunchy element and intensified spice. Serve with toasted bread and a drizzle of olive oil to complete the dining experience.

9. **Variations and Tips**

- **Spice it Up:** For a more intense flavor, add a pinch of chili powder during cooking for a mild heat.
- **Add Veggies:** If you prefer a more substantial version, add diced potatoes along with the carrots to make the soup even more filling.
- **Tomato Twist:** Adding canned diced tomatoes during cooking can add an acidic note and a vibrant color to the soup.
- **Vegan Option:** Ensure the vegetable broth is gluten-free for a vegan and gluten-free version. Substitute cream with coconut milk or cashew cream for a delicate, slightly sweet note without dairy.
- **Experiment with Spices:** Try adding turmeric for an earthy and slightly bitter taste, along with a beautiful golden color. If you enjoy a smoky flavor, add some smoked paprika during the sauté.
- **Creamy Finish:** Add a spoonful of Greek yogurt when serving for a creamy contrast to the spiced soup.

Wild Vegetable Soup

Wild Vegetable Soup has ancient origins and was popular in various rural communities across Europe. During the Middle Ages, it was often prepared using vegetables gathered from forests and gardens, representing a humble yet flavorful and hearty example of rustic cuisine. In some regions, such as the Alpine areas, villagers would forage for nettles and wild herbs to create nourishing soups that provided essential nutrients during harsh winters. This comforting dish is perfect for warming both body and soul on cold winter days.

Preparation Time: 20 minutes

Total Time: 1 hour

Servings: 4

Ingredients

- 3 tablespoons extra virgin olive oil
- 1 large onion
- 3 garlic cloves
- 3 carrots
- 1 leek
- 2 medium potatoes
- 3 celery stalks
- 1 bunch Swiss chard
- 7 ounces (200 g) fresh nettles (or spinach)

- 6 cups (1.5 liters) vegetable broth
- 2 bay leaves
- 2 sprigs fresh thyme
- Salt and pepper, to taste
- Fresh parsley, chopped for garnish
- Grated lemon zest (optional)

Instructions:

1. **Prepare Ingredients**: Peel and finely chop the onion and garlic. Peel the carrots and potatoes, then cut them into roughly 1/2-inch (1 cm) cubes. Clean the leek and slice it thinly. Chop the celery stalks into 1/2-inch (1 cm) pieces. Wash the Swiss chard and cut it into thin strips. If using nettles, wear gloves to avoid irritation and rinse well under cold water. This preparation ensures all ingredients are ready for a smoother cooking process.

2. **Sauté**: In a large pot, heat the extra virgin olive oil over medium heat. Add the chopped onion and sauté for about 5-7 minutes until golden and fragrant. Add the chopped garlic and cook for another minute, being careful not to burn it. Add the leek and celery, cooking for another 5 minutes while stirring frequently. This step develops a rich and aromatic base for the soup.

3. **Add Vegetables**: Add the carrots and potatoes to the pot, cooking for 5-7 minutes and stirring occasionally. Add the Swiss chard and nettles, stirring until they start to wilt. These wild greens add an authentic rustic flavor reminiscent of traditional dishes.

4. **Cook the Soup**: Pour in the hot vegetable broth, then add the bay leaves and thyme sprigs. Bring the mixture to a boil, then reduce the heat and cover the pot. Let it simmer for about 30-35 minutes, or until all the vegetables are tender. Stir occasionally, adding 1/2 to 1 cup (120-240 ml) of broth or hot water if needed to maintain the desired consistency. Slow cooking allows the flavors to meld, resulting in a flavorful and nutritious soup.

5. **Season**: Once all vegetables are cooked, remove the bay leaves and thyme sprigs. Season with salt and pepper to taste. If desired, add a squeeze of lemon juice and a bit of grated lemon zest just before serving to add a fresh and vibrant note to the dish, balancing the natural sweetness of the vegetables.

6. **Blend (Optional)**: For a smoother texture, blend part of the soup using an immersion blender, leaving some chunks for added texture. For a more rustic consistency, simply skip this step.

7. **Serve**: Serve the soup hot in rustic bowls, garnished with chopped fresh parsley and a drizzle of extra virgin olive oil. You can also add toasted bread croutons for some extra crunch. If desired, rub the croutons with a garlic clove for extra flavor. This soup is perfect as a main dish or a hearty appetizer, ideal for cold evenings with its rich and comforting flavors.

8. **Presentation** Presentation is key to making the soup inviting. Garnish each bowl with some fresh parsley and a drizzle of olive oil for added shine and flavor. Place a toasted slice of bread on the side of the bowl for a rustic touch that completes the culinary experience. For a crunchy and visually appealing element, add toasted pumpkin seeds on top. To create a truly unique experience, consider using rustic dishware or handmade ceramic bowls to evoke a medieval atmosphere. You can often find such dishware at local craft fairs, antique shops, or even online retailers. For affordable alternatives, try using simple ceramic bowls with an earthy finish. Wild Vegetable Soup is ideal for sharing in a convivial setting, accompanied by red wine or herbal teas to complete the meal.

9. **Variations and Suggestions:**

   - **Add Legumes**: To make the soup even more nourishing, consider adding legumes such as white beans or chickpeas during cooking. This will make the soup more filling and nutritious.
   - **Seasonal Vegetables**: You can vary the vegetables according to the season: kale or wild spinach make great additions.
   - **Spicy Touch**: For a spicier flavor, add a pinch of chili powder or smoked paprika during the sauté step.
   - **Mushrooms**: Add fresh mushrooms, sautéing them with the onion to add an earthy flavor to the dish.
   - **Creamy Version**: For a creamier version, stir in a small amount of heavy cream at the end of cooking and mix well to combine all flavors.

First Courses

Introduction: Origins and Reinterpretation of Medieval First Courses

Medieval first courses were substantial, often forming the cornerstone of the meal. Envision a rustic kitchen where a large pot over an open fire simmers slowly, mingling the scents of grains and legumes with the fresh aromas of herbs. These hearty dishes were central to the communal dining experience, offering both warmth and sustenance to help individuals face their daily challenges. During times when food was primarily a source of energy and sustenance for long days of labor in fields or artisanal workshops, these dishes were crafted with readily available ingredients like grains, legumes, and seasonal vegetables. Staples such as spelt, barley, and wheat were commonly used. Homemade pastas, often dressed with simple herb-based sauces or rich meat broths, were typical. Soups, particularly those based on grains and legumes, provided a comprehensive and nutritious meal, easily adaptable to the varying seasons and the availability of ingredients.

These first courses were often made in large quantities to feed entire families, necessitating considerable skill and patience in their preparation. This not only facilitated a bond between the cook and those who partook of the meals but also fostered a sense of community and shared experience. Furthermore, these dishes held symbolic significance beyond their nutritional value. Recipes handed down through generations encapsulated both cultural and familial heritage, transforming meal preparation into a communal and historical act.

Aromatic herbs like rosemary, thyme, and sage, cultivated in small kitchen gardens, infused these dishes with distinctive flavors, evoking the natural landscapes from which they were harvested. Grains were often roasted before cooking to deepen their flavor, with each family having its unique methods of preparing fresh pasta, which varied in shape and texture depending on regional and local traditions. Thus, medieval cuisine was a direct reflection of available resources, daily necessities, and regional diversity, also serving as an avenue for expressing culinary creativity and ingenuity.

In the kitchens of the nobility, first courses were luxurious, incorporating exotic spices such as saffron, cinnamon, and nutmeg, along with almond milk and fine meats like venison or peacock. Elaborate dishes like 'blancmange'—a chicken and almond concoction—or spiced soups enriched with unique flavors were not uncommon. These preparations played a crucial role in showcasing the wealth and refinement of the host at grand banquets, with first courses often presented with great elaboration to impress guests. Conversely, in peasant homes, first courses were simpler yet robust, commonly consisting of grain soups, legume pottages, and pasta dressed with whatever the season offered. Stale bread was frequently employed to thicken these soups, enhancing their satiety factor.

The regional variations of these first courses mirrored the local availability of ingredients, fostering a rich diversity of flavors and culinary practices across different areas. Each locale had its specialties, influenced by climate and local cultural practices, contributing to a rich and varied gastronomic tradition. Additions like lentils, chickpeas, and beans further enriched these dishes, boosting their nutritional content and making them more substantial.

Today, we reinterpret these medieval first courses to align with modern tastes and dietary preferences, blending authenticity with contemporary cooking techniques. While medieval soups utilized dense broths and rustic ingredients, today's versions are prepared with lighter broths and refined cooking methods to enhance flavors without the heaviness. We continue to incorporate whole grains and fresh pasta but introduce lighter cooking techniques and modern ingredients to enrich the flavors while maintaining the integrity of the dishes. The use of fresh herbs and spices is carefully balanced to make each recipe suitable for contemporary palates, maintaining a connection with their historical roots. Techniques like steam cooking and the use of lighter broths make the dishes more digestible while preserving their authentic, rustic essence. This section aims to streamline preparation times, making these historical recipes more accessible for everyday cooking, offering a culinary experience that merges authenticity and innovation. These first courses celebrate the simple yet intense flavors of the past while providing a contemporary reinterpretation that makes these recipes enjoyable and practical for modern kitchens. We also encourage customization of the recipes, allowing for experimentation with local and seasonal ingredients, much like medieval cooks would have done, enhancing culinary creativity and adapting to what is currently available, staying true to the spirit of medieval cooking traditions.

Tria di Vermicelli (Vermicelli Tria)

Originating from Sicily, Tria di Vermicelli has its roots in medieval cuisine influenced by the Arab domination of the island. During the Arab rule in Sicily (827-1091), many culinary techniques and ingredients, such as saffron, almonds, and innovative pasta-making methods, were introduced, greatly enriching Sicilian cuisine. This dish is an example of how simple ingredients can create an elegant preparation, combining almond milk and saffron to create a unique and sophisticated flavor typical of medieval noble tables.

Preparation Time: 20 minutes

Total Time: 1 hour

Servings: 4

Ingredients:

- 10.5 ounces (300 g) vermicelli
- 4 cups (1 liter) unsweetened almond milk (preferably homemade for an authentic flavor)
- 1 packet saffron
- 1 tablespoon extra virgin olive oil
- Salt, to taste
- Freshly ground black pepper, to taste
- Grated Parmesan cheese, for garnish (optional)
- Chopped parsley, for garnish
- 1 teaspoon nutmeg (optional)

42

- Grated lemon zest (optional)

Instructions:

1. **Prepare Almond Milk**: If you prefer to make almond milk at home, start by grinding about 5.3 ounces (150 g) of almonds and mixing them with 4 cups (1 liter) of water. Strain the mixture through a cotton cloth or fine-mesh sieve to obtain smooth almond milk. You can skip this step if using store-bought almond milk. Homemade almond milk will add greater freshness and authenticity to the recipe, along with a more intense flavor due to the absence of preservatives and the freshness of the almonds.

2. **Prepare Cooking Base**: In a large pot, heat the almond milk over medium heat. Add the saffron and stir until fully dissolved, giving the milk a rich golden color. Season with salt and bring to a light boil. Stir occasionally to prevent the milk from sticking to the bottom of the pot. For a more aromatic flavor, you can also add a teaspoon of nutmeg, which adds a spicy note that pairs well with the almond milk and saffron, and some grated lemon zest.

3. **Cook Vermicelli**: Once the almond milk begins to boil, add the vermicelli. Cook the pasta in the milk, stirring frequently to prevent sticking. Cook for about 10-12 minutes, until the vermicelli are al dente. If needed, add hot water to adjust the consistency of the cooking liquid, ensuring the pasta remains immersed in the milk for a creamy and even texture.

4. **Season**: When the vermicelli are cooked, transfer them to serving plates. Drizzle with extra virgin olive oil for added shine and a richer flavor. Add freshly ground black pepper to balance the sweetness of the almond milk. If desired, sprinkle with a small amount of grated Parmesan cheese to deepen the flavor. Consider adding a light sprinkle of lemon zest for freshness and an aromatic contrast.

5. **Serve**: Serve the Tria di Vermicelli hot, garnished with grated Parmesan cheese for a more robust flavor if desired. For a touch of freshness, add chopped parsley. The parsley not only adds color but also balances the sweetness of the almond milk. This dish can be accompanied by a light white wine, such as Pinot Grigio or Soave, or an herbal tea like chamomile or lemon balm to complete the medieval culinary experience. You can also decorate the plate with some grated lemon zest for an extra touch of freshness and a visually appealing presentation.

6. **Suggestions and Variations**:

   - **Add Spices**: You can personalize the dish by adding spices like nutmeg, which was highly appreciated in medieval kitchens.
   - **Add Herbs**: For a more flavorful version, you can add herbs like thyme during cooking.
   - **Substitute Pasta**: If vermicelli are not available, you can substitute with thin spaghetti or angel hair pasta, which have a similar texture and work well in this preparation.

- **Add Dried Fruits**: Another interesting variation could be the addition of chopped dried fruits, such as almonds, to add crunchiness and make the dish even more nutritious.

Ravioli Verdi (Green Ravioli)

Ravioli Verdi originate from the northern regions of Italy, particularly Emilia-Romagna, known for its rich culinary heritage. This region is famous for its fresh pasta dishes and the use of leafy green vegetables like spinach and Swiss chard, which have long been integral to its traditional cuisine. These ravioli exemplify how simple yet fresh and local ingredients can be combined to create an elegant and flavorful dish.

Preparation Time: 30 minutes

Total Time: 1 hour 30 minutes

Servings: 4

Ingredients:

- **For the pasta:**
    - 10.5 ounces (300 g) all-purpose flour
    - 2 eggs
    - 3.5 ounces (100 g) fresh spinach
    - A pinch of salt
- **For the filling:**
    - 9 ounces (250 g) fresh ricotta

- o 3.5 ounces (100 g) boiled and squeezed Swiss chard

- o 1.8 ounces (50 g) grated Parmesan cheese

- o Salt and pepper, to taste

- o Nutmeg, to taste

- **For the sauce:**

  - o 1.8 ounces (50 g) butter

  - o 8-10 fresh sage leaves

  - o Grated Parmesan cheese, for garnish

Instructions:

1. **Prepare the Green Pasta**: Start by boiling the spinach in hot water for a few minutes until softened. Drain and squeeze out as much water as possible to prevent the dough from becoming too wet. Finely chop the spinach and set it aside. In a large bowl, sift the flour and create a well in the center. Add the eggs, the pinch of salt, and the chopped spinach. Knead until a smooth and elastic dough is formed. If needed, add a bit more flour to prevent the dough from being too sticky. Form the dough into a ball, cover it with plastic wrap, and let it rest for at least 20 minutes. This resting period allows the gluten to relax, improving the dough's elasticity and making it easier to roll out. This resting period is important to allow the gluten to relax, making the dough more elastic and easier to roll out.

2. **Prepare the Filling**: Meanwhile, prepare the filling. In a bowl, mix the ricotta with the boiled and finely chopped Swiss chard. Add the grated Parmesan cheese, a pinch of salt, pepper, and a dash of nutmeg. Mix well until creamy and well combined. Ensure the filling is dry enough to prevent it from leaking out during cooking. If the filling is too moist, add a bit of breadcrumbs to maintain its consistency. A well-prepared filling will ensure the ravioli hold together during cooking, providing a balanced taste experience.

3. **Roll Out the Dough**: After resting, divide the dough into two portions. Using a rolling pin or a pasta machine, roll each portion into a thin sheet, about 1-2 mm thick. Try to achieve two sheets of similar size for easier ravioli preparation. During rolling, lightly dust the work surface and rolling pin with flour to prevent sticking. You may use a pasta machine for a more even and thin sheet, ensuring an ideal consistency for the ravioli. Roll the dough thinly, as thick dough will result in heavy, unevenly cooked ravioli.

4. **Form the Ravioli**: On one sheet, place small amounts of filling (about one teaspoon each) at regular intervals, leaving enough space between portions. Cover with the second sheet and press well around the filling to seal the edges, making sure to expel any air. Use a pasta cutter

or a knife to cut the ravioli. Lightly dust with flour to prevent sticking. For a better seal, you can press the edges lightly with a fork, creating a decorative pattern. Properly sealing the ravioli is essential to prevent the filling from escaping during cooking.

5. **Cook the Ravioli**: Bring a large pot of salted water to a boil. Use about 10 g of salt per liter of water. Cook the ravioli for about 3-4 minutes, or until they float to the surface. Drain gently with a slotted spoon to avoid breaking them. To prevent sticking, gently stir the ravioli while cooking, as this is the preferred method to ensure they do not stick together without affecting the sauce's ability to adhere. Do not overcrowd the pot: cook in small batches to ensure the ravioli cook evenly.

6. **Prepare the Sauce**: In a large skillet, melt the butter over medium-low heat. Add the sage leaves and let them sizzle for a few minutes until the butter turns golden and aromatic. Add the drained ravioli and gently toss in the sage butter for a couple of minutes, ensuring they are well coated. Be gentle to keep the ravioli intact. Sage butter is a classic pairing for ravioli, but you could also experiment with other flavors, such as brown butter with chopped nuts for added crunch, or a light sprinkle of grated lemon zest for a fresh contrast to the richness of the butter.

7. **Serve**: Serve the ravioli hot, garnished with grated Parmesan cheese for extra flavor. For freshness, add chopped parsley. This dish pairs well with a dry white wine, such as Vermentino or Pinot Grigio, to enhance the delicate flavors. If you prefer a non-alcoholic option, pair with a fresh herbal tea, such as thyme or sage, to echo the dish's aromatic notes. Serve the ravioli immediately to enjoy their soft texture and rich filling, or keep warm for a few minutes in a low-temperature oven if needed.

8. **Variations and Suggestions:**

   - **Leafy Greens**: Substitute Swiss chard with other leafy greens, such as kale or nettles, for a different flavor.

   - **Dairy-Free Version**: Use silken tofu instead of ricotta and omit the Parmesan for a dairy-free version.

   - **Herbs**: Enrich the filling with herbs like thyme or oregano for an extra aromatic note.

   - **Chopped Nuts**: Add chopped nuts, like walnuts, to the filling for a crunchy texture and more complex flavor.

   - **Cream and Mushroom Sauce**: Prepare a light cream and porcini mushroom sauce to pour over the ravioli before serving for a richer dish with contrasting flavors and textures.

Gnocchi Medievali di Formaggio (Medieval Cheese Gnocchi)

Gnocchi Medievali di Formaggio originate from the mountainous regions of central Italy, where fresh goat cheese was often used in rustic culinary preparations. This dish represents a perfect blend of simple and genuine flavors, with a soft texture that highlights the rich and delicate taste of the cheese. Goat cheese was commonly used in these mountainous regions due to its availability and the ease of raising goats in rugged terrain, making it a staple in many traditional dishes. The cheese's tangy, slightly earthy flavor complements the simplicity of the ingredients, adding a rich depth to the gnocchi while maintaining a delicate balance that highlights the rustic quality of the dish.

Preparation Time: 25 minutes

Total Time: 1 hour

Servings: 4

Ingredients:

- 14 ounces (400 g) fresh goat cheese

- 5.3 ounces (150 g) all-purpose flour

- 2 egg yolks

- A pinch of salt

- Nutmeg, to taste

- 1.8 ounces (50 g) butter

- 8-10 fresh sage leaves

- Grated Parmesan cheese, for garnish

- Freshly ground black pepper (optional)

Instructions:

1. **Prepare the Dough**: Start by preparing the dough for the gnocchi. In a large bowl, crumble the fresh goat cheese using a fork or potato masher. Make sure the cheese is well crumbled to avoid lumps in the dough. Add the egg yolks, a pinch of salt, and a generous grating of nutmeg. Mix well with a spatula until smooth. You can also use a manual whisk to ensure the yolks are well incorporated and the mixture is even. Gradually add the sifted flour, kneading with your hands until a soft but firm dough is formed. It is helpful to use a lightly floured wooden board for kneading: this helps achieve a more uniform consistency and prevents sticking. The dough should not be too sticky, but should remain soft to give the gnocchi a delicate texture. If the dough is too wet, add more flour, one tablespoon at a time, until the right consistency is reached. To check the consistency, press the dough gently with a finger: it should feel elastic but not sticky. Use a bench scraper to gather any dough remnants and keep the work area clean throughout the kneading process. Once the dough is ready, cover it with a clean cloth and let it rest for 10-15 minutes, allowing the flour to fully hydrate and the ingredients to blend better. This resting time is crucial for making the gnocchi softer and easier to shape.

2. **Shape the Gnocchi**: Transfer the dough to a lightly floured work surface. Divide the dough into portions and roll each portion into cylinders about 3/4 inch (2 cm) thick. Cut the cylinders into small pieces, about 3/4 inch (2 cm) long, to form the gnocchi. If desired, roll each gnocchi over the tines of a fork to create the characteristic ridges that help hold the sauce. Lightly dust the gnocchi with just enough flour to prevent them from sticking together while you work, being careful not to use too much flour as it could alter the texture of the gnocchi.

3. **Cook the Gnocchi**: Bring a pot of salted water to a boil. Gentle stirring is the preferred method to prevent the gnocchi from sticking, as adding oil to the water can alter the sauce's ability to adhere to the gnocchi. Once the water reaches a boil, carefully drop in the gnocchi, a few at a time, to avoid overcrowding the pot. Cook the gnocchi until they float to the surface, about 3-4 minutes. Once cooked, drain gently with a slotted spoon and transfer to a large bowl.

4. **Prepare the Sauce**: In a large skillet, melt the butter over medium-low heat. Add the fresh sage leaves and let them sizzle for a few minutes, until the butter turns golden and aromatic. Sage butter is a simple yet flavorful sauce, perfect for enhancing the delicate taste of cheese

gnocchi. Cook over low heat to avoid burning the butter, which could result in a bitter taste. If desired, add a pinch of freshly ground black pepper for a slight hint of spice.

5. **Sauté the Gnocchi**: Add the drained gnocchi to the skillet with the sage butter. Sauté gently for 2-3 minutes, allowing the gnocchi to absorb the butter and sage flavors. Stir carefully to avoid breaking the gnocchi, as they are quite delicate. Ensure that each gnocchi is well coated with the sauce for a consistent flavor.

6. **Serve**: Serve the gnocchi hot, garnished with a generous sprinkle of grated Parmesan cheese and, if desired, freshly ground black pepper. Gnocchi Medievali di Formaggio are perfect paired with a dry white wine, such as Vermentino or Pinot Grigio, which balances the richness of the cheese and butter. Alternatively, try an herbal tea like chamomile or lemon balm for a non-alcoholic option that complements the rustic flavors of the dish. If you prefer a non-alcoholic option, an herbal tea such as thyme or sage pairs well with the rustic flavors of the dish.

7. **Variations and Suggestions**

   - **Fresh Herbs**: Add chopped fresh herbs like parsley or chives to the dough for a more aromatic flavor.
   - **Creamy Sauce**: For a richer version, add a bit of heavy cream to the sage butter to create a creamy sauce.
   - **Smoked Cheese**: Substitute part of the goat cheese with smoked ricotta for a more intense, rustic flavor.
   - **Chopped Nuts**: Add chopped nuts, such as walnuts, almonds, or hazelnuts, to the sauce for a crunchy element.
   - **Make Ahead**: Prepare the gnocchi in advance and store them on a floured tray covered with plastic wrap in the refrigerator until ready to cook.

Lasagne alla Corte Medievale (Lasagna at the Medieval Court)

Lasagne alla Corte Medievale find their origins in the kitchens of Italian courts, particularly in central and northern Italy, where recipes were enriched with precious ingredients and fine spices, such as saffron and cloves, which were highly prized in medieval cooking. This reinterpretation of medieval lasagna combines rustic and refined flavors, perfect for a convivial table.

Preparation Time: 30 minutes

Total Time: 1 hour 30 minutes

Servings: 6

Ingredients:

- 10.5 ounces (300 g) fresh lasagna sheets
- 14 ounces (400 g) ground meat (beef and pork mix)
- 1 finely chopped onion
- 2 minced garlic cloves
- 2 finely chopped carrots
- 2 finely chopped celery stalks
- 14 ounces (400 g) tomato puree
- 2/3 cup (150 ml) red wine
- 1 bay leaf
- 1 sprig fresh thyme
- 1.8 ounces (50 g) butter

- 4 tablespoons extra virgin olive oil
- 2 cups (500 ml) béchamel sauce
- 3.5 ounces (100 g) grated Parmesan cheese
- Salt, to taste
- Freshly ground black pepper, to taste

Instructions:

1. **Prepare the Ragù**: In a large skillet, heat the extra virgin olive oil over medium heat. Add the chopped onion, garlic, carrots, and celery. Sauté for about 10 minutes, until the vegetables are soft and slightly golden. Add the ground meat and cook until well browned, about 8-10 minutes, breaking up any lumps with a wooden spoon. Let the meat absorb the flavors of the vegetables, cooking for another 5 minutes and stirring frequently.

2. **Deglaze with Wine**: Pour the red wine into the skillet and let it evaporate completely for about 5 minutes, stirring well. This will add depth and richness to the flavor of the ragù. Once the wine has evaporated, add the tomato puree, bay leaf, and thyme sprig. Cover and let cook over low heat for about 40-50 minutes, stirring occasionally to prevent the ragù from sticking to the bottom of the skillet. The ragù is ready when it is thick, the flavors are well combined, and the oil starts to separate from the sauce. Season with salt and pepper towards the end of cooking, ensuring the flavors are well balanced.

3. **Prepare the Béchamel Sauce**: Meanwhile, prepare the béchamel sauce if not already made. In a small saucepan, melt the butter over medium heat and slowly add the flour, stirring constantly with a whisk to prevent lumps. Gradually pour in the warm milk, continuing to stir until the béchamel thickens and reaches a velvety consistency. Add a pinch of salt and, if desired, a grating of nutmeg for extra flavor. The béchamel should be thick enough to coat the back of a spoon, with a smooth, velvety texture that doesn't run off too quickly.

4. **Assemble the Lasagna**: Preheat the oven to 350°F (180°C). If using a convection oven, reduce the temperature to 320-340°F (160-170°C) to avoid overcooking. In a baking dish, spread a thin layer of ragù to prevent the lasagna sheets from sticking to the bottom. Arrange a layer of lasagna sheets, then cover with a layer of ragù and a layer of béchamel. Sprinkle with some grated Parmesan cheese. Repeat the process until all the ingredients are used, finishing with a layer of béchamel and a generous sprinkling of Parmesan. Make sure each layer is evenly distributed for a consistent and flavorful result.

5. **Bake**: Cover the baking dish with aluminum foil to prevent the surface from drying out too quickly and bake for about 30 minutes. Remove the foil and bake for another 15-20 minutes, until the surface is golden and crisp. For an even more flavorful crust, add a few pats of butter on the surface before removing the foil. Let the lasagna rest for at least 10-15 minutes before serving, allowing the flavors to meld together.

6. **Serve**: Serve the lasagna hot, accompanied by a fresh green salad with ingredients such as arugula, cherry tomatoes, and shaved fennel, dressed with a light lemon vinaigrette to balance the richness of the dish. These lasagna are perfect for a Sunday family lunch or a convivial dinner with friends. Leftover lasagna can be stored in the refrigerator for 2-3 days or frozen for later use. The ideal pairing is with a full-bodied red wine, such as Chianti or Montepulciano, which enhances the intense and rustic flavors. You can also garnish the dish with a few fresh thyme leaves for a touch of color and added aroma.

7. **Variations and Suggestions**

   - **Vegetarian Version**: Replace the meat with a mix of vegetables such as mushrooms, zucchini, and eggplant, optionally adding legumes for more texture.

   - **Mozzarella Addition**: For a richer touch, add cubed mozzarella between the layers, which will melt and make the lasagna even creamier and more flavorful.

   - **Spicy Twist**: Add spices like smoked paprika or cayenne pepper for a spicier version.

   - **White Wine Option**: Substitute red wine with white wine for a lighter, fresher flavor profile in the ragù.

   - **Crunchy Element**: Experiment with adding chopped nuts, such as almonds, for a crunchy texture and unique flavor.

Spelt and Legume Soup

Spelt and legume soup has ancient origins, typical of the rural areas of central Italy. This rustic and nutritious dish was very common in medieval farming communities, where it was made with simple but flavorful and substantial ingredients. In medieval times, spelt was one of the most commonly cultivated grains, providing a hearty base for many dishes, while legumes like chickpeas and lentils were valued for their protein content, making them essential staples for sustaining energy during hard labor. The combination of spelt and legumes provided a balanced meal that was both filling and highly nutritious, offering a source of carbohydrates, fiber, and protein. This dish is a testament to the resourcefulness of rural communities, using what was available to create satisfying meals that nourished both body and spirit.

Preparation Time: 20 minutes

Total Time: 1 hour 15 minutes

Servings: 6

Ingredients:

- 1 cup pearled spelt (200 g)
- 1 cup dried chickpeas (or canned) (150 g)
- 3/4 cup lentils (150 g)
- 1 finely chopped onion
- 2 chopped carrots
- 2 chopped celery stalks

- 3 minced garlic cloves
- 4 tablespoons extra virgin olive oil
- 6 1/3 cups vegetable broth (1.5 liters)
- 2 bay leaves
- 1 sprig fresh rosemary
- Salt, to taste
- Freshly ground black pepper, to taste
- Fresh chopped parsley, for garnish

Instructions:

1. **Prepare the Ingredients**: If using dried chickpeas, soak them in cold water for at least 8 hours (or overnight). Drain and rinse well before using. Rinse the spelt under cold running water and let it drain. Lentils do not need soaking, but it is advisable to rinse them before use. These preliminary steps will ensure even cooking and better consistency of the soup. Taking the time to properly prepare the ingredients will also help bring out the natural flavors of the spelt and legumes, making the final dish even more enjoyable.

2. **Vegetable Sauté**: In a large pot, heat the extra virgin olive oil over medium heat. Add the chopped onion, garlic, carrots, and celery. Sauté for about 10 minutes, until the vegetables are soft and slightly golden. Stir every 1-2 minutes to prevent sticking and burning. This sauté forms the aromatic base of the soup and helps build a deep, rich flavor. For a more intense flavor, you can add a small amount of chopped chili pepper to the sauté. The aromas released during this step will set the stage for the hearty flavors that follow, filling your kitchen with a comforting, inviting scent.

3. **Add the Legumes and Spelt**: Add the chickpeas (if dried, pre-cooked), lentils, and spelt to the pot. Mix well to combine all the ingredients and let them toast for 2-3 minutes. Toasting the spelt helps to lightly caramelize the grains, sealing in the starches, which results in a better texture during cooking. This step also adds a slightly toasted note to the overall flavor of the dish, making the soup more interesting and complex. The caramelization enhances the nutty qualities of the spelt, and the toasting process helps to infuse the legumes with a deeper, more robust flavor.

4. **Slow Cooking**: Pour the hot vegetable broth into the pot, ensuring all ingredients are completely covered. Add the bay leaves and rosemary sprig. Bring to a boil (about 5-7 minutes), then reduce the heat and cover the pot with a lid. Let the soup simmer over low heat for about 50-60 minutes, stirring occasionally. If necessary, add more broth or hot water, 1/4 cup at a time, to maintain the desired consistency. During cooking, the aroma of the herbs will fill the kitchen, creating a warm and inviting atmosphere. The slow cooking process allows the flavors to meld beautifully, creating a soup that is rich and comforting, perfect for a cozy evening.

5. **Adjust Seasoning**: Remove the bay leaves and rosemary sprig from the pot. Adjust salt and pepper to taste, tasting to check the flavor. For a creamier consistency, blend part of the legumes with an immersion blender, leaving the rest intact. This step will help give the soup a thicker, velvety texture, making it particularly comforting on cold winter days. Blending part of the soup also enhances the cohesion of the flavors, creating a harmonious balance between the different ingredients.

6. **Rest the Soup**: Once cooking is complete, turn off the heat and let the soup rest for about 10 minutes. This resting time allows the flavors to meld together, making the soup even tastier. You can prepare the fresh parsley for garnish and make sure the bread is toasted and ready to serve. The resting period is essential, as it allows the flavors to fully develop and ensures that each bite is packed with the richness of the herbs, legumes, and spelt.

7. **Serve**: Serve the soup hot, garnished with a drizzle of raw extra virgin olive oil and a sprinkle of fresh chopped parsley. For a different twist, try adding grated lemon zest or a pinch of chili flakes for extra flavor. For an extra touch, accompany the soup with slices of rustic toasted bread, rubbed with a garlic clove for added flavor. The toasted bread not only adds a pleasant crunch but also helps balance the creaminess of the soup, making each bite more interesting. This hearty dish is perfect for sharing with family or friends, offering warmth and comfort during colder months.

8. **Variations and Suggestions**

   - **Additional Legumes**: Add cannellini or borlotti beans to increase the protein content and variety of flavors. The addition of different legumes not only boosts the nutritional value but also adds different textures, making the soup more satisfying.
   - **Tomato Paste**: For a richer version, add a few tablespoons of tomato paste for a touch of acidity. The tomato paste will deepen the color of the broth and add a pleasant tang that complements the earthiness of the spelt and legumes.
   - **Leafy Greens**: Add spinach or kale during the last 10 minutes of cooking to enrich the soup with essential nutrients and a hint of freshness. The greens will wilt beautifully into the soup, adding both color and a fresh, slightly bitter note that balances the richness of the legumes.
   - **Vegan Version**: Use only vegetable broth and garnish with olive oil without cheese for a completely vegan version. You can also add nutritional yeast for a cheesy flavor without dairy, making it a great option for those avoiding animal products.
   - **Herb Variations**: Experiment with different herbs such as thyme or sage in place of rosemary for a different aromatic profile. Each herb will bring its own unique character to the soup, allowing you to customize the dish based on your preferences.

9. **Storage**: If you have leftovers, spelt and legume soup keeps well in the refrigerator for 2-3 days. Make sure to let it cool completely before storing it in an airtight container. When

reheating, add some broth or water to reach the desired consistency, as the soup tends to thicken as it rests. This soup is also suitable for freezing, so you can make a larger batch and freeze some for a quick and nutritious meal in the future. When reheating from frozen, thaw the soup in the refrigerator overnight and then warm it slowly on the stove, adding additional liquid as needed to maintain the perfect consistency. Having this soup on hand can be a lifesaver on busy weeknights when you need a wholesome meal in minutes.

10. **Utensil Tips**: For this recipe, it is helpful to have a large pot with a thick bottom, which distributes heat evenly and prevents the risk of burning the sauté. An immersion blender is recommended for those who want a creamier consistency. Also, a good sharp kitchen knife will make vegetable preparation easier, resulting in more precise and safe cuts. If possible, use a wooden spoon for stirring, as it is less abrasive on the bottom of the pot and helps avoid scratches during cooking. A ladle with a pouring lip is also useful for serving, as it allows you to transfer the soup into bowls neatly without spills. Proper utensils not only make the cooking process smoother but also enhance the overall experience of making and serving this delicious soup.

Tagliatelle with Venison Ragù

Tagliatelle with venison ragù is a traditional dish from the mountainous areas of northern Italy, where game meat was widely used in cooking due to the abundance of wild game in the alpine regions. This dish celebrates the rustic and intense flavors of alpine culinary traditions, combining the tenderness of fresh pasta with the rich taste of venison, which has long been a staple of local cuisine.

Preparation Time: 30 minutes

Total Time: 2 hours

Servings: 4

Ingredients:

- 14 oz fresh egg tagliatelle (400 g)
- 1.1 lbs minced venison (500 g)
- 1 finely chopped onion
- 2 chopped carrots
- 2 chopped celery stalks
- 3 minced garlic cloves
- 4 tablespoons extra virgin olive oil
- 1 glass red wine (approx. 5 fl oz or 150 ml)
- 14 oz tomato passata (400 g)
- 2 bay leaves

- 1 sprig fresh thyme
- Salt, to taste
- Freshly ground black pepper, to taste
- Grated Parmigiano Reggiano, for serving
- Fresh thyme leaves or lemon zest, for garnish (optional)

Instructions:

1. **Prepare the Ingredients**: Begin by preparing all the vegetables for the soffritto. Finely chop the onion, carrots, celery, and garlic to create a smooth and well-combined ragù. Use a sharp knife to ensure uniform pieces, which will help create a consistent texture in the final dish. Proper preparation is key to achieving the depth of flavor that makes this ragù so special.

2. **Vegetable Sauté**: In a large pot, heat the extra virgin olive oil over medium heat. Add the chopped onion, garlic, carrots, and celery, and sauté for about 10-12 minutes, until the vegetables become soft and slightly golden. Stir often to prevent sticking. This soffritto forms the aromatic base of the ragù and will add depth to the flavor of the venison. The sautéed vegetables release their natural sweetness, which balances the rich and earthy flavor of the venison. For an even deeper flavor, you can let the vegetables caramelize slightly, taking care not to burn them.

3. **Cook the Venison**: Add the minced venison to the pot with the sautéed vegetables. Increase the heat slightly and allow the meat to brown for about 10 minutes, stirring occasionally to prevent sticking. It's important that the meat browns well, as this step will help develop the rich flavors of the ragù. The venison should have a light golden crust, which adds a toasted flavor to the final dish. To achieve this crust, avoid overcrowding the pan to ensure the meat browns properly. Browning the meat properly enhances the savory flavors and creates a complex base for the ragù.

4. **Deglaze with Red Wine**: Pour the glass of red wine into the pot, stirring well to deglaze the bottom. Let it cook for 5 minutes, or until the alcohol has evaporated. The red wine adds acidity and complexity to the ragù, balancing the robust flavors of the venison. Be sure to use a good quality wine, such as Chianti or Barolo, as its flavor will directly impact the final result. The deglazing process also helps to release any caramelized bits stuck to the bottom of the pot, incorporating them into the sauce for added flavor.

5. **Add the Tomato Passata**: Add the tomato passata, bay leaves, and thyme sprig. Mix well, reduce the heat to low, and cover the pot with a lid. Let the ragù simmer gently for about 1 hour and 15 minutes, stirring every 15-20 minutes. Partially cover the pot to help control the consistency, allowing steam to escape while retaining moisture. During this time, the flavors will meld together, and the meat will become tender. The slow cooking process allows the flavors to fully develop, resulting in a rich, hearty sauce. If the ragù becomes too dry, you

can add a little broth or hot water to maintain the right consistency. The gentle simmering helps break down the venison, making it tender and allowing it to absorb all the flavors from the herbs and vegetables.

6. **Adjust Seasoning**: Remove the bay leaves and thyme sprig from the pot. Adjust the seasoning with salt and pepper to taste, ensuring the flavors are balanced. The ragù should have a slight acidity from the tomato and wine, while the depth of flavor comes from the venison and aromatic herbs. Taste the sauce at this stage and adjust as needed, adding more salt or pepper if necessary to achieve a well-rounded flavor. The seasoning should enhance the natural taste of the venison without overpowering it.

7. **Cook the Tagliatelle**: Bring a large pot of salted water to a boil and cook the fresh egg tagliatelle according to the package instructions (usually 3-4 minutes). Drain the pasta, reserving a ladle of cooking water. Fresh pasta cooks quickly, so keep an eye on it to ensure it does not overcook. The reserved cooking water contains starch that will help bind the sauce to the pasta, creating a cohesive dish.

8. **Assemble the Dish**: Add the cooked tagliatelle directly to the pot with the ragù. Gently toss to combine, adding some reserved cooking water if needed to achieve a creamy, well-coated consistency. The ragù should fully envelop the tagliatelle without being too runny. The cooking water helps emulsify the sauce, giving it a silky texture that clings to the pasta. Take care not to overmix, as fresh pasta can be delicate and may break apart if handled too roughly.

9. **Serve**: Serve the tagliatelle with venison ragù hot, garnished with a generous sprinkle of grated Parmigiano Reggiano. For an added touch, you can decorate with a few fresh thyme leaves or freshly grated lemon zest to add brightness and balance to the dish. Pair the dish with a robust red wine that complements the intense flavors of the ragù, such as a Barolo or a Brunello di Montalcino. The richness of the sauce is beautifully complemented by the salty Parmigiano and the freshness of the lemon zest, creating a well-balanced and satisfying meal.

10. **Variations and Suggestions**

   - **Alternative Meats**: If you cannot find venison, substitute with wild boar or a mix of beef and pork for an equally rich flavor. Wild boar has a similar gamey quality to venison, while beef and pork provide a more familiar, yet still hearty, flavor profile.

   - **Creamy Version**: For a milder version, add a small amount of heavy cream during the last 10 minutes of cooking to make the ragù creamier. The cream will soften the acidity of the tomatoes and add a luxurious texture to the sauce.

   - **Make Ahead**: You can prepare the ragù in advance—it will taste even better the next day, as the flavors have more time to meld together. Store it in an airtight container in the refrigerator for up to three days, or freeze it for longer storage. Reheat gently on the stove, adding a bit of water or broth to loosen the sauce if needed.

- **Vegetable Alternatives**: Substitute celery with fennel or leeks to add a different layer of flavor to the soffritto. Fennel will add a subtle anise-like sweetness, while leeks provide a milder, more delicate onion flavor.

- **Herb Variations**: Experiment with different herbs, such as rosemary or sage, in place of thyme to give the ragù a different aromatic profile. Rosemary pairs well with game meats, adding a woody, fragrant note, while sage gives a warm, earthy flavor.

Pappardelle with Hare Sauce

Pappardelle with hare sauce is a traditional dish from medieval Tuscan cuisine, known for its rich and intense flavor. During the Middle Ages, hare was often hunted in the Tuscan countryside and provided a valuable source of protein for rural communities. This dish combines the tenderness of fresh pasta with the depth of the sauce, offering a rustic and authentic gastronomic experience typical of medieval feasts.

Preparation Time: 40 minutes

Total Time: 3 hours and 30 minutes

Servings: 4

Ingredients:

- 14 oz fresh egg pappardelle (400 g)
- 1.76 lbs hare (preferably leg), cut into pieces (800 g)
- 1 finely chopped onion
- 2 chopped carrots
- 2 chopped celery stalks
- 3 minced garlic cloves
- 1/3 cup red wine (100 ml)
  - lbs tomato passata (500 g)
- bay leaves
- sprigs rosemary

- tablespoons extra virgin olive oil
- 1 glass vegetable or meat broth (approx. 5 fl oz or 150 ml)
- 1 tablespoon tomato paste
- 1 pinch nutmeg
- Salt, to taste
- Freshly ground black pepper, to taste
- Grated Parmigiano Reggiano, for serving

Instructions:

1. **Marinate the Hare**: Before cooking, marinate the hare pieces in a bowl with the red wine, a few bay leaves, and a sprig of rosemary for at least 2 hours (preferably overnight). This step helps to reduce the gamey flavor of the meat and makes it more tender. Drain the hare from the marinade and pat it dry with paper towels, reserving the wine for cooking. Marination is crucial for developing a deep aromatic profile and will make the sauce more balanced.

2. **Prepare the Ingredients**: Finely chop the onion, carrots, celery, and garlic for the soffritto. Preparing the vegetables in this way will help meld the flavors together and create a rich aromatic base for the hare sauce. Use a sharp knife for uniform chopping and even cooking. It is recommended to prepare all ingredients in advance to make the cooking process smoother.

3. **Vegetable Sauté**: In a large pot, heat the extra virgin olive oil over medium heat. Add the onion, garlic, carrots, and celery, and sauté for about 10-12 minutes, until the vegetables become soft and slightly golden. Stir the vegetables frequently to prevent burning. This step is crucial for developing the base flavor of the dish and building a solid foundation for the sauce.

4. **Cook the Hare**: Add the hare pieces to the pot with the sautéed vegetables and brown for 10-15 minutes over medium-high heat, turning occasionally for an even sear. This step is important to seal the juices of the meat and add an intense flavor. The browning should be even and golden on all sides to achieve a flavorful and well-structured sauce.

5. **Deglaze with Wine**: Pour the reserved red wine marinade into the pot to deglaze, scraping up the concentrated flavors left by the meat. Cook for 5-7 minutes until the alcohol has evaporated, stirring well. Be sure to scrape the bottom of the pot to incorporate all the caramelized bits, which will impart a deep and complex flavor to the sauce.

6. **Add Tomato Passata and Herbs**: Add the tomato passata, broth, tomato paste, bay leaves, rosemary sprigs, and a pinch of nutmeg. Reduce the heat to low, cover the pot with a lid, and let it simmer gently for about 2 and a half hours, stirring occasionally. During cooking, the hare will become tender, and the sauce will thicken, developing a rich and aromatic flavor.

Gradually add the broth, about half a glass at a time, if needed, to maintain a creamy but not overly thick consistency.

7. **Adjust the Seasoning**: Remove the bay leaves and rosemary sprigs from the sauce. Adjust the seasoning with salt and pepper to taste. If the sauce is too thick, add a bit of broth to achieve the desired consistency. If it's too runny, continue cooking uncovered over medium heat to evaporate the excess liquid. This step ensures the perfect consistency for the sauce, allowing it to cling well to the pappardelle.

8. **Cook the Pappardelle**: Bring a large pot of salted water to a boil and cook the fresh egg pappardelle according to the package instructions (usually 3-4 minutes). Drain the pasta al dente, reserving a ladle of cooking water. The starchy cooking water can be used to better bind the pasta to the sauce.

9. **Assemble the Dish**: Add the pappardelle directly to the pot with the hare sauce. Gently toss to combine the pasta with the sauce, adding a bit of cooking water to make everything creamier. It's important to mix gently to avoid breaking the pappardelle and to ensure that each strand is well coated with the sauce.

10. **Serve**: Serve the pappardelle with hare sauce hot, garnished with a generous sprinkle of grated Parmigiano Reggiano. For a finishing touch, add a few fresh rosemary leaves and a drizzle of extra virgin olive oil to enhance the flavors. This dish pairs perfectly with a full-bodied red wine, such as Chianti or Montepulciano d'Abruzzo, which balances the rich and intense flavors of the hare sauce. Serve with rustic toasted bread for dipping or accompany with grilled polenta for a different twist.

11. **Variations and Suggestions**

   - **Meat Alternatives**: If hare is not available, substitute it with rabbit, which has a milder flavor but a similar texture.
   - **Richness**: For a richer sauce, add some smoked pancetta during the sauté step to introduce a smoky depth of flavor.
   - **Make Ahead**: The sauce can be made in advance and reheated when serving—resting allows the flavors to meld even better, resulting in an even more delicious dish.
   - **Vegetarian Version**: Use fresh porcini mushrooms instead of hare to create an equally hearty and flavorful sauce.
   - **Herb Variations**: Experiment with different herbs like sage or thyme to provide a different aromatic profile to the dish.

Main Courses

Introduction: Origins and Reinterpretation of Medieval Main Courses

Medieval main courses often featured richly flavored meats, game, and fish, enhanced by spicy and aromatic sauces. In noble courts, banquets were prime opportunities to display wealth and power, as seen in the lavish feasts of the Medici court in Florence, known for their extravagance and abundance. These banquets were significant events, organized for weddings, religious and political celebrations, or the visits of distinguished guests, where every detail reflected the host's opulence. This was evident in the preparation of elaborate dishes made from fine meats such as deer, boar, and duck, often cooked with expensive spices sourced from distant lands like black pepper, saffron, and cloves. Freshwater fish like trout and eels also played a vital role during the lean days mandated by the religious rules of the time. These dishes were designed to impress guests and create an atmosphere of lavishness, where every element on the table underscored the host's power and generosity.

The cooking techniques used for these main courses were often complex, involving open fires, spits, and large iron or terracotta pots. Meats were slow-cooked to achieve a tender and succulent texture, while sauces were crafted with spices, dried fruits, and vinegar to balance sweet and savory flavors. These dishes were meant to be shared at banquets held for religious festivals, political celebrations, or significant events, where conviviality and opulence were central themes. Conviviality was an integral part of medieval culture, and communal meals served to strengthen social and political bonds. Techniques like smoking and salting were common for preserving meats to ensure a food supply during difficult times, such as winter. The use of spices, besides enhancing flavor, often helped mask the taste of less fresh foods, a necessity in the absence of refrigeration. Spices were seen as a symbol of prestige, and their inclusion in noble dishes was a clear statement of status.

In peasant homes, however, main courses were simpler, focusing on local and accessible ingredients like chicken, rabbit, and fish caught in nearby streams. Aromatic herbs such as rosemary, sage, and thyme were used to season meats, while moist cooking methods were often employed to create rich and flavorful dishes even from modest ingredients. Pork fat was a staple, used both for cooking and preserving, adding flavor to simpler dishes. In these households, meals were a time of sharing, and the kitchen reflected the economy of the home: nothing was wasted, and every ingredient was maximized. Food was often cooked in large common pots, and slow cooking helped extract maximum flavor from available ingredients. Even in these settings, the use of local herbs and spices added depth of flavor to the dishes, making them tastier despite the simplicity of the ingredients.

In the modern reinterpretation of medieval main courses, we strive to maintain the authenticity and richness of flavors, adapting them to contemporary tastes and culinary techniques. Game has been replaced with more readily available meats like beef and chicken, and practical cooking methods such as ovens and barbecues are used to replicate the flavors of open fire. Spices are carefully balanced to suit modern palates, which are less accustomed to the extreme contrasts of sweet and savory typical of medieval cuisine. The modern reinterpretations aim to retain the rustic and flavorful essence of the dishes, but with a lighter and more accessible approach that suits contemporary living. We also explore the use of spices that were less common today but highly valued in medieval times, such as mace and juniper, offering a taste of the era's aromatic complexity without overwhelming the dish.

Sauces, which in medieval times were often thick and heavily spiced, have been lightened. However, we continue to use dried fruits like almonds and walnuts, and vinegar to evoke the typical acidity of the period. The goal is to create main courses that are both faithful to historical traditions and enjoyable to eat, without being overly heavy or complex in preparation. Techniques such as braising or low-temperature cooking are employed to achieve tender and flavorful meats, similar to the original preparations. The use of sous-vide, a modern cooking technique where food is vacuum-sealed and cooked at low temperatures in hot water, represents a modern innovation that allows us to replicate the tenderness of slowly cooked meats without the need to monitor the cooking for hours. The sous-vide method not only ensures perfect texture but also better preserves the nutrients and flavors of the ingredients, aligning perfectly with the intent to maximize each element of the dish.

Additionally, vegetarian variants have been introduced to adapt medieval recipes to current dietary needs. Although dishes based on legumes and vegetables were less common at the time, they can provide an interesting and tasty alternative to traditional meat-based main courses. By using ingredients like mushrooms, legumes, and grains, we can recreate the essence of medieval dishes in a lighter version suitable for modern eating habits, without sacrificing the flavor and aromatic depth characteristic of the cuisine of the era. Mushrooms, in particular, are chosen for their earthy flavor and meaty texture, which make them an excellent substitutein meat-heavy dishes. Legumes such as lentils and chickpeas add a significant nutritional component. The vegetarian variants include dishes like mushroom stews with nuts and bean casseroles with aromatic herbs, offering a complex and satisfying flavor while maintaining a connection to the historical roots of medieval cuisine.

This section of the book presents a variety of reinterpreted recipes ranging from meat and fish to vegetarian alternatives, with the goal of reviving the flavors and traditions of medieval cuisine in a modern key. Among the recipes featured are spiced beef braised with dried fruit, a contemporary reinterpretation of classic venison salmi, and a richly flavored mushroom and legume casserole as a vegetarian alternative. The main courses we propose are designed to be enjoyed both in a family setting as part of a convivial meal and on special occasions, to recreate the atmosphere of a true medieval banquet but with the practicality and lightness required by contemporary times. The presentation of the dishes has been carefully considered to add a visual touch that can impress diners, just as it was during medieval banquets, but with a modern aesthetic that emphasizes simplicity and elegance. Each recipe is conceived not only as a dish to be enjoyed but also as a visual and sensory experience that transports the diner on a journey through time, between history and modernity. Decorative elements used in the presentation, such as fresh herbs, dried fruit, and rustic tableware, recall the medieval aesthetic, adding an additional layer of authenticity to the culinary experience. The preparations are designed to highlight the value of sharing and hospitality, two fundamental aspects of medieval culture, reinterpreted in a modern key to unite tradition and innovation.

Roast Lamb with Rosemary and Garlic

This roast lamb recipe, originating from the countryside of Tuscany, embodies the simplicity and richness of the flavors typical of medieval cuisine. In the Middle Ages, the use of aromatic herbs like rosemary and garlic, combined with slow roasting, was common both in noble court feasts and in rural family meals. At feasts, the meal was a moment of display and celebration, while in rural homes, it represented an occasion for sharing and community warmth.

Preparation Time: 30 minutes

Total Time: 2 hours and 30 minutes

Servings: 4

Ingredients:

- 3.3 lbs leg of lamb (1.5 kg)
- 6 garlic cloves
- 4 sprigs fresh rosemary
- 2 tablespoons extra virgin olive oil
- Coarse salt, to taste
- Freshly ground black pepper, to taste
- 3/4 cup dry white wine (200 ml)
- A little less than 1/2 cup vegetable or lamb broth (100 ml)
- 1 sprig fresh thyme (optional)
- 1 sprig fresh sage (optional)

- Grated lemon zest, for serving (optional)

Instructions:

1. **Prepare the Lamb**: Preheat the oven to 180°C (350°F). Pat the leg of lamb dry with paper towels to help achieve a good sear during roasting. Use a sharp knife to make deep incisions on the surface of the meat, deep enough to insert garlic cloves. This will help distribute the flavors evenly during cooking. In the Middle Ages, such techniques were essential to ensure that the meat was well-seasoned using the limited resources available.

2. **Season the Meat**: Peel the garlic cloves and cut them in half. Insert each half clove into the incisions made in the lamb, along with sprigs of rosemary. Rub the lamb with extra virgin olive oil, coarse salt, and freshly ground black pepper to help the seasoning penetrate better, making the meat more flavorful. For a more intense flavor, marinate the lamb for 1-2 hours at room temperature or up to 12 hours in the refrigerator. This marination process was also used in medieval times to soften tougher meats and ensure greater depth of flavor.

3. **Initial Searing**: Heat a large, oven-safe skillet over medium-high heat. Place the leg of lamb in the skillet and sear for about 4-5 minutes per side, until it has an even golden-brown crust. The meat should have a deep golden crust without burning, ensuring it is well-sealed and flavorful. Use kitchen tongs to turn the meat without piercing it, to retain the internal juices. This stage will give the meat an outer crispiness that will perfectly balance its internal tenderness. In medieval times, searing over an open flame was key to creating a flavorful crust and trapping the meat's juices.

4. **Roast in the Oven**: Once seared, pour the white wine into the skillet, scraping the bottom with a wooden spatula to release the caramelized bits. Let the wine evaporate for a couple of minutes, then add the vegetable or lamb broth. Cover the skillet with a lid or aluminum foil to retain moisture, ensuring that the meat remains tender during the long cooking process, and transfer it to the preheated oven. Roast the lamb for about 1 hour and 45 minutes, basting it every 30 minutes with the cooking liquid. If necessary, add more broth to keep the meat moist. Add fresh thyme and sage during the last 30 minutes for an extra layer of flavor. The slow oven roasting is a modern interpretation of traditional medieval spit-roasting or hearth cooking, but the principle remains the same: the meat must cook slowly to become tender and flavorful.

5. **Rest the Meat**: Remove the lamb from the oven and let it rest for at least 15 minutes before slicing. Cover with aluminum foil during resting to keep it warm and allow the juices to redistribute within the meat, ensuring a soft and juicy texture. This step is crucial and was also practiced in medieval times, albeit with different methods, to allow the meat to stabilize and become more flavorful.

6. **Serve**: Slice the lamb into thick pieces and arrange them on a serving platter. Strain the remaining cooking liquid through a fine-mesh sieve to obtain a smooth sauce, removing any solids and ensuring a refined texture. Drizzle the lamb slices with the sauce and serve hot. This roast pairs perfectly with rustic sides such as roasted potatoes, grilled vegetables, or a legume puree, which echo the authentic flavors of medieval cuisine. You can also add a sprinkle of grated lemon zest for a fresh touch. In medieval times, the dish was often accompanied by seasonal vegetables and legumes, which were staple elements of the daily diet.

7. **Variations and Suggestions**

- **Herbs**: For a richer flavor, add thyme and sage during roasting.
- **Sweet Note**: Add halved onions or whole carrots along with the broth and wine for a natural sweetness.
- **Lighter Version**: Substitute the lamb with a whole chicken, reducing the cooking time to about 1 hour and 15 minutes.
- **Fresh Finish**: Add chopped fresh parsley before serving for a bright touch. In medieval times, local and seasonal ingredients were often added to personalize the recipe based on availability, a practice that remains relevant today to make the dish even more delicious and sustainable.

Country Sausage (Saucisse à Cuire)

Country sausage, known in France as "Saucisse à Cuire," originates from the countryside of Burgundy, where it was made with simple, local ingredients, using pork seasoned with spices and herbs. This recipe embodies the tradition of rustic, home-style medieval cooking, when preserving meat and making the most of available ingredients were vital for rural families.

Preparation Time: 40 minutes

Total Time: 1 hour and 20 minutes

Servings: 4

Ingredients:

- 1.76 lbs ground pork (half shoulder, half belly) (800 g)
- 2 garlic cloves
- 1 tablespoon fennel seeds
- 1 teaspoon freshly ground black pepper
- 1 teaspoon coarse salt
- 1 tablespoon dry white wine
- Natural sausage casing
- 2 tablespoons extra virgin olive oil
- 1 large onion
- 2 bay leaves
- A little less than 1 cup meat broth (200 ml)

71

Instructions:

1. **Prepare the Meat**: Start by grinding the pork, or if you've purchased pre-ground meat, ensure it is well mixed. Peel and finely chop the garlic, then add it to the meat. Also add the fennel seeds, black pepper, salt, and white wine. Mix everything thoroughly with your hands to evenly distribute the flavors. Let the mixture rest covered in the refrigerator for at least 30 minutes to allow the flavors to meld. If you have the time, let it rest for up to 24 hours for a more intense flavor.

2. **Prepare the Casing**: While the meat rests, prepare the natural sausage casing. Rinse it well under running water and soak it in lukewarm water for about 20 minutes. This step helps to remove any residual salt and makes the casing more flexible, making it easier to fill. Ensure the casing is thoroughly cleaned and entirely free of any residue to ensure a smoother texture and prevent imperfections during cooking, such as tears or uneven cooking.

3. **Fill the Casing**: Using a sausage funnel or a sausage stuffer, begin to fill the casing with the meat mixture. Be sure to leave some space in the casing, avoiding overfilling to prevent the sausage from bursting during cooking. Once filled, tie the casing at regular intervals to form sausages of about 10-12 cm each. You can use kitchen twine to ensure the knots are secure. To prevent the sausages from breaking during cooking, prick them gently in several places with a needle to allow steam to escape. Let the sausages rest for at least 20 minutes at room temperature before cooking.

4. **Brown the Sausages**: In a large skillet, preferably cast iron for better heat distribution, heat the extra virgin olive oil over medium heat. Add the sausages and brown them for about 5-6 minutes, turning them on all sides until they are evenly golden. This step is essential to seal the juices inside the sausages, ensuring they remain juicy and flavorful. Sealing the juices keeps the meat tender and prevents it from drying out, enhancing both the flavor and texture. Cast iron is ideal for achieving perfect browning because of its ability to maintain a consistent temperature and distribute heat evenly.

5. **Slow Cooking**: Once the sausages are browned, add the thinly sliced onion, bay leaves, and meat broth to the skillet. Cover with a lid and cook over low heat for about 30-35 minutes. During cooking, make sure to turn the sausages every 10-15 minutes and baste them with the cooking liquid to keep them moist and full of flavor. If necessary, add more broth to prevent the pan from drying out. Covering with a lid helps retain moisture and ensures even cooking, preventing the sausages from drying out.

6. **Rest and Serve**: Once cooked, remove the sausages from the skillet and let them rest for a few minutes before serving. This step allows the juices to redistribute within the meat, ensuring a more tender and flavorful result. Serve the sausages hot, accompanied by the caramelized onions and the cooking juices, which will have acquired a rich and aromatic

flavor. Alternatively, serve them with roasted potatoes or a simple salad, such as mixed greens with a light vinaigrette or roasted root vegetables, to offer a variety of options to diners. These sausages are perfect when served with mashed potatoes, grilled vegetables, or a rustic cabbage salad for an authentic touch. You can also add roasted vegetables as a side dish to further enrich the meal and make the presentation more appealing.

7. **Variations and Suggestions**

- **Herbs**: For a more intense flavor, add fresh herbs such as thyme or marjoram to the meat mixture.
- **Wine Alternative**: Substitute the white wine with a bit of cider for a fruity note that pairs well with pork.
- **Spicy Version**: Add a pinch of crushed red pepper to the meat mixture for a slightly spicier sausage.
- **Rustic Touch**: Cook the sausages on a barbecue for a smoky flavor and irresistible crispiness.
- **Mustard Sauce**: Serve with a mustard and honey sauce to add a pleasant sweetness and a contrasting spicy kick, balancing the meat's flavor perfectly.
- **Side Dish**: Pair the sausages with rustic bread, lightly toasted for added crunch to the meal.

Grilled Fish with Yellow Sauce (Poivre Jaunet)

This recipe has its origins in the medieval cuisine of the Burgundy region in France, where sauces made with spices and refined aromas were often used to enhance the delicate flavor of fish. The yellow sauce, or "Poivre Jaunet," takes its name from the golden hue provided by saffron, and was a sign of refinement on noble tables of the time.

Preparation Time: 45 minutes

Total Time: 1 hour and 30 minutes

Servings: 4

Ingredients:

- 4 fillets of white fish (sea bass, cod, or trout)
- 2 tablespoons extra virgin olive oil
- Salt and pepper, to taste

For the Yellow Sauce (Poivre Jaunet):

- 3/4 cup fish stock (200 ml)
- A little less than 1/2 cup dry white wine (100 ml)
- 1 teaspoon saffron
- 1 teaspoon mild mustard
- 1.8 oz cold butter, cut into cubes (50 g)
- 1 teaspoon coarsely ground black pepper

74

- 1 tablespoon lemon juice
- Salt, to taste

Instructions:

1. **Prepare the Fish**: Preheat the grill or a grill pan over medium-high heat. Ensure it's hot enough to get a good sear, as a hot grill helps develop flavor and prevents the fish from sticking. Pat the fish fillets dry with paper towels, then brush them with extra virgin olive oil and season with salt and pepper. This step helps create a crispy crust and prevents the fish from sticking to the grill. Place the fillets on the grill skin-side down. Cook for 4-5 minutes per side, or until the flesh becomes opaque and easily flakes with a fork. If necessary, use a spatula to gently turn the fillets without breaking them. Transfer the fish to a plate and cover with aluminum foil to keep it warm. Let the fish rest for about 5 minutes to allow the juices to redistribute evenly, keeping it tender and juicy.

2. **Prepare the Yellow Sauce (Poivre Jaunet)**: In a small saucepan, bring the fish stock and white wine to a boil. Stir well to combine and ensure the wine flavor fully integrates into the stock. Let it simmer for about 10 minutes, reducing the liquid by half. This reduction process concentrates the flavors, making the sauce richer and more flavorful. Add the saffron and mustard, stirring well to achieve an even golden color. Saffron not only provides color but also imparts a subtle floral aroma that enhances the dish's profile. Reduce the heat to low and add the cold butter, one cube at a time, stirring constantly to incorporate it and create a smooth, creamy sauce. It is important to add the butter gradually to prevent the sauce from separating and to maintain a silky texture. Do not let the sauce boil after adding the butter, as this could cause it to curdle and ruin the desired creamy texture. Add the black pepper and lemon juice, adjusting salt as needed. The black pepper adds a subtle kick, while the lemon juice balances the richness of the butter with a pleasant acidity.

3. **Assembly and Serving**: Arrange the fish fillets on a serving platter. Garnish the plate with lemon slices or fresh herbs like parsley or thyme for a pop of color. Pour the yellow sauce over each fillet, distributing it evenly. Ensure each portion is well-covered to guarantee a flavorful bite every time. Serve immediately, garnishing with a few threads of saffron or a sprinkle of black pepper for a visual touch. Distribute the garnish evenly for an elegant finish. This detail adds a touch of sophistication, making the dish perfect for a special occasion. Accompany the dish with grilled vegetables or roasted potatoes for a complete meal with a medieval-inspired twist. Choose seasonal vegetables like zucchini, bell peppers, or asparagus, which will add freshness and crunch to the dish.

4. **Variations and Suggestions**

- **Fish Choice**: This recipe can be adapted to other types of fish like salmon or sea bass, depending on availability and personal preference. Salmon, for example, will add a richer and oilier note, perfect for those who enjoy bold flavors.
- **Vegan Option**: During sauce preparation, substitute butter with vegetable margarine and use vegetable broth instead of fish stock for a vegan version. Follow the same steps, making sure to add the margarine gradually for a creamy consistency.
- **Flavor Enhancer**: If you prefer a more intense sauce, add a pinch of turmeric along with the saffron during preparation to amplify both the color and aromatic profile. Turmeric also adds a slightly earthy flavor that pairs well with fish.
- **Complete Meal**: Consider adding a fresh salad with lemon vinaigrette or a side of white beans with aromatic herbs for a fuller meal. These pairings not only complete the dish but offer a variety of textures and flavors that complement each other well.
- **Elegant Presentation**: For a more refined presentation, serve the fish on a bed of vegetable puree, like a pea velouté or a ginger-infused carrot cream. This adds an interesting visual and gustatory element, elevating the dish to a gourmet level.

Chicken in Almond Sauce

This traditional dish hails from medieval Spain, where almonds were commonly used in cooking, particularly in sauces that showcased both Moorish and European influences. The combination of tender chicken with a rich almond sauce evokes the rustic and refined flavors of a bygone era, perfect for any occasion where you want to bring a touch of history to the table.

Preparation Time: 30 minutes

Total Time: 1 hour 15 minutes

Servings: 4

Ingredients:

- **Chicken**

    - 4 chicken thighs, skin-on
    - 3 tablespoons extra virgin olive oil
    - Salt and pepper, to taste

- **For the Almond Sauce**

    - 1 medium onion, finely chopped
    - 2 garlic cloves, minced
    - 3.5 oz blanched almonds (100 g)
    - 3/4 cup chicken broth (200 ml)
    - A little less than 1/2 cup dry white wine (100 ml)

- o 1 teaspoon saffron threads
- o 1 tablespoon white wine vinegar
- o 1 teaspoon honey
- o Fresh parsley, finely chopped, for garnish

Instructions:

1. **Prepare the Chicken:** Heat the extra virgin olive oil in a large skillet over medium-high heat. Pat the chicken thighs dry with paper towels—this will help achieve a crispy skin. Season generously with salt and freshly ground black pepper. Once the oil is hot, add the chicken thighs, skin side down, and sear them for 5-6 minutes on each side until golden brown and crispy. This step not only adds color but also helps to lock in the moisture, ensuring tender chicken. Remove the chicken from the skillet and set aside on a plate.

2. **Make the Almond Sauce:** In the same skillet, add the finely chopped onion, reducing the heat to medium. Cook the onion for about 5 minutes until it turns translucent. This step creates the foundation for the sauce's flavor. Add the minced garlic and sauté for an additional 2 minutes, being careful not to burn it, as burnt garlic can turn bitter. Stir in the blanched almonds and toast them for 3-4 minutes, stirring constantly. Toasting the almonds enhances their flavor and gives the sauce a nuttier, richer taste. Pour in the white wine, stirring well to deglaze the pan and release any browned bits stuck to the bottom—these bits add depth to the sauce. Allow the alcohol to cook off for 2-3 minutes. Add the chicken broth and saffron, stirring to combine. Bring the mixture to a boil, then reduce the heat and let it simmer for 10 minutes, allowing the saffron to infuse the sauce with its golden color and subtle aroma.

3. **Cook the Chicken in the Sauce:** Return the seared chicken thighs to the skillet, nestling them into the almond sauce. Ensure the chicken is mostly submerged to allow for even cooking and full absorption of the sauce's flavors. Cover the skillet with a lid and cook over low heat for 30-35 minutes, or until the chicken is cooked through and tender. Turn the chicken occasionally during cooking, spooning the sauce over it to keep the skin flavorful.

4. **Finish the Sauce:** Once the chicken is cooked, carefully remove it from the skillet and set it aside. To the simmering sauce, add the white wine vinegar and honey, stirring well to create a balance of acidity and sweetness—this is a hallmark of medieval flavors, where a balance of sweet and sour was often sought. Season the sauce with additional salt and pepper, if needed. For a smooth, creamy consistency, use an immersion blender to purée the sauce. If you prefer a more rustic texture, leave the almonds whole for added crunch. This choice allows for versatility depending on the desired final presentation.

5. **Assemble and Serve:** Return the chicken thighs to the skillet, spooning the almond sauce over the top to coat them evenly. Let the chicken simmer in the sauce for an additional 5 minutes over low heat, which helps meld the flavors together. Transfer the chicken to a serving dish, pour the sauce over the top, and garnish with freshly chopped parsley. The

vibrant green parsley adds a pop of color and freshness that balances the richness of the dish. Serve immediately, accompanied by crusty rustic bread to soak up the almond sauce or with seasonal grilled vegetables to complement the flavors and textures of the dish.

6. **Variations and Suggestions**

- **Chicken Substitutes**: You can substitute the chicken thighs with boneless chicken breasts or even turkey for a leaner option. Adjust cooking times accordingly to prevent the meat from drying out.

- **Richer Sauce**: For a creamier almond sauce, stir in 50 ml of fresh cream during the final stages of sauce preparation. This addition will make the sauce extra luxurious, perfect for a special dinner.

- **Spiced Almonds**: For added warmth, you can toast the almonds with a hint of cinnamon or nutmeg before incorporating them into the sauce. These spices add a layer of complexity and aroma that pairs beautifully with the chicken.

- **Suggested Side Dishes**: This dish pairs wonderfully with a side of rice pilaf or couscous, which can absorb the rich almond sauce. Alternatively, serve it with mashed potatoes for a comforting, hearty option.

Beef Stew with Spices

This recipe has its origins in the culinary tradition of Andalusia, a region in southern Spain, during the Middle Ages. The combination of meat and dried fruit was very popular, influenced by the Arab domination. The rich and creamy almond sauce gives a unique flavor to the beef, making this dish particularly suitable for banquets and special occasions.

Preparation Time: 30 minutes

Total Time: 3 hours

Servings: 6

Ingredients:

- 2.2 lbs (1 kg) beef (shoulder or shank), cut into cubes
- 3 tablespoons (45 ml) extra virgin olive oil
- Salt and pepper to taste
- 2 large onions, chopped
- 3 garlic cloves, minced
- 2 carrots, sliced
- 2 celery stalks, chopped
- 2 bay leaves
- 1 teaspoon (5 g) ground cinnamon
- 1 teaspoon (5 g) ground cloves
- 1 teaspoon (5 g) ground ginger

- 1 teaspoon (5 g) allspice
- 2 cups (500 ml) beef broth
- 1 cup (200 ml) red wine
- 1 tablespoon (15 ml) red wine vinegar
- 1 teaspoon (5 ml) honey
- Fresh parsley, chopped for garnish

Instructions:

1. **Prepare the Meat**: In a large casserole, heat the extra virgin olive oil over medium-high heat. Browning the meat is important as it develops a richer flavor through the Maillard reaction, which enhances the overall depth of the stew. Season the beef cubes with salt and pepper, then sear them in the casserole, turning for about 5-7 minutes until evenly browned. Transfer the meat to a plate and set aside.

2. **Vegetable Sauté**: In the same casserole, add the chopped onions and sauté for about 5 minutes until softened and golden. Add the minced garlic and continue cooking for another 2 minutes. Add the carrots and celery, stirring well, and cook for another 5 minutes.

3. **Add the Spices**: Add the cinnamon, cloves, ginger, and allspice. These spices were commonly used in medieval Andalusian cuisine, contributing to a distinctive flavor that reflects the Arab influences of the era. Stir well to combine the spices with the vegetables and let cook for 1-2 minutes until they release their aroma.

4. **Cook the Stew**: Return the beef to the casserole along with the bay leaves. Pour in the red wine and let the alcohol evaporate for a couple of minutes, stirring occasionally to ensure the wine flavor balances without being too strong. Add the beef broth, cover the casserole, and reduce the heat to low. Let the stew simmer for about 2 hours and 30 minutes, stirring occasionally. The meat should become very tender and flavorful.

5. **Finish the Stew**: Add the red wine vinegar and honey, stirring well to balance the flavors. The acidity of the vinegar and the sweetness of the honey combine to enhance the complexity of the flavors, creating a harmonious contrast that enriches the stew's depth. Adjust salt and pepper if needed. Let the stew cook uncovered for another 15-20 minutes, allowing the liquids to reduce and the sauce to thicken.

6. **Assemble and Serve**: Remove the bay leaves from the stew. Serve the stew hot, garnished with chopped fresh parsley. Accompany with rustic bread or polenta for a complete meal with a medieval flavor.

7. **Variations and Suggestions**

   - **Substitute Meats**: You can substitute the beef with lamb or pork for different flavors. Lamb will add a richer and more gamey note to the dish.

- **Adjust Spices**: If you prefer a less spicy taste, reduce the amount of cinnamon and cloves. You can also add a pinch of smoked paprika for a different touch.
- **Serving Suggestions**: This stew pairs well with mashed potatoes or a side of roasted vegetables. You can also serve it with a spiced pilaf rice for a more elaborate experience.
- **Different Cooking Methods**: For added convenience, you can prepare this stew in a slow cooker. After browning the meat and sautéing the vegetables, transfer everything to the slow cooker and cook on low for 6-8 hours.
- **Additional Garnishes**: Add some toasted almonds on top for a crunch that complements the creamy sauce, or serve with a dollop of yogurt to balance the spices.

Sweet and Sour Rabbit

This sweet and sour rabbit recipe has its origins in Sicily and is a traditional dish of Southern Italian cuisine, where sweet and sour flavors were often used due to Arab influence. The raisins and pine nuts, common ingredients in Sicilian cuisine due to Arab influences, add a delicate sweetness that perfectly contrasts with the acidity of the vinegar, creating a dish rich in balanced flavors and history. Rabbit, a meat traditionally appreciated in the rural areas of Sicily, was often cooked in this way to celebrate special occasions and to showcase local ingredients.

Preparation Time: 25 minutes

Total Time: 2 hours

Servings: 4

Ingredients:

- 2.5 lbs (1.2 kg) rabbit, cut into pieces
- 4 tablespoons extra virgin olive oil
- Salt and pepper, to taste
- 1 large onion, finely chopped
- 3 garlic cloves, minced
- 1/2 cup (100 g) raisins
- 1/3 cup (50 g) pine nuts
- 3/4 cup (200 ml) red wine vinegar
- 2 tablespoons honey

- 3/4 cup (200 ml) dry white wine
- 1 1/4 cups (300 ml) beef or chicken broth
- 1 sprig rosemary
- 2 bay leaves
- 1 teaspoon ground cinnamon
- Fresh parsley, chopped, for garnish

Instructions:

1. **Prepare the Rabbit:** In a large casserole, heat the extra virgin olive oil over medium-high heat. Season the rabbit pieces with salt and pepper, then brown them in the casserole for about 8-10 minutes, until golden brown on all sides. This helps develop a deeper flavor through the Maillard reaction and seals in the juices, enhancing the overall richness of the dish. Transfer the rabbit to a plate and set aside.

2. **Prepare the Sweet and Sour Base:** In the same casserole, add the chopped onion and sauté for about 5 minutes until translucent. Add the minced garlic and cook for another 2 minutes, stirring to prevent burning. Add the raisins and pine nuts, stirring for 2-3 minutes until the pine nuts are lightly toasted and the raisins have softened. This creates a rich, complex sweet and sour base, with the pine nuts adding a nutty note and the raisins balancing the acidity of the vinegar.

3. **Flavor and Reduce:** Pour the red wine vinegar into the casserole and let it reduce for 2-3 minutes, allowing the alcohol to evaporate and the acidity to concentrate for a more balanced flavor. Add the honey, stirring well to ensure it dissolves completely into the sauce. The vinegar and honey work together to create the characteristic sweet and sour balance, a hallmark of Sicilian cuisine.

4. **Cook the Rabbit:** Return the rabbit pieces to the casserole and pour in the white wine. This helps deglaze the casserole, incorporating all the browned bits from the bottom and adding additional flavor to the sauce. Let the alcohol evaporate for a couple of minutes, then add the broth, rosemary sprig, bay leaves, and cinnamon. Bring to a boil, then reduce the heat to low, cover, and let the rabbit simmer for about 1 hour and 30 minutes, or until tender and fully cooked. Stir every 20-30 minutes to ensure the rabbit is well infused with the flavors of the sauce. Slow cooking allows the meat to absorb all the aromas and become extremely tender and flavorful.

5. **Assemble and Serve:** Remove the rosemary sprig and bay leaves from the casserole. Adjust salt and pepper if needed. Transfer the rabbit to a serving dish and cover it with the sweet and sour sauce. Garnish with fresh chopped parsley and serve immediately. This dish pairs well with rustic bread, polenta, or roasted potatoes to help absorb the delicious sauce. You

can also add a few orange slices or fresh rosemary sprigs for decoration, adding a touch of freshness, color, and aroma.

6. **Variations and Suggestions:**

- **Alternative Meats**: If preferred, you can substitute the rabbit with chicken or guinea fowl. Adjust cooking times accordingly to ensure optimal results.
- **Bolder Flavor**: Add a pinch of ground cloves along with the cinnamon for a more complex aromatic profile.
- **Side Pairings**: This dish goes well with grilled vegetables or celery root puree for a creamy and delicate contrast.
- **Serving Bread**: Rustic bread is ideal for "fare la scarpetta," the Italian tradition of mopping up the sauce from the plate, highlighting the importance of the flavorful sauce.
- **Ingredient Substitutes**: For an even more authentic touch, use homemade wine vinegar or replace raisins with dried apricots for a slightly different fruity note.
- **Mediterranean Twist**: For a more elaborate dish, add black olives during the last 30 minutes of cooking, contributing to the Mediterranean flavors of the dish.

Duck with Prune Sauce

This duck with prune sauce dish has its origins in the rural regions of Southwestern France, particularly in the Périgord area, where the combination of duck and dried fruits was typical of the peasant cuisine during the Middle Ages. Prunes, often used to preserve fruit for the winter, add a sweetness that perfectly balances the rich flavor of the duck, creating a delightful contrast that enhances the rustic character of this dish.

Preparation Time: 20 minutes

Total Time: 1 hour 45 minutes

Servings: 4

Ingredients:

- 1 whole duck (about 3.3 lbs / 1.5 kg)
- 3 tablespoons extra virgin olive oil
- Salt and pepper, to taste
- 1 medium onion, finely chopped
- 3 garlic cloves, minced
- 7 oz (200 g) pitted prunes
- 3/4 cup (200 ml) red wine
- 3/4 cup (200 ml) chicken broth
- 2 tablespoons red wine vinegar
- 1 teaspoon ground cinnamon

- 1 teaspoon honey
- 1 sprig fresh thyme
- Zest of 1 orange
- Fresh parsley, chopped, for garnish

Instructions:

1. **Prepare the Duck:** Preheat the oven to 350°F (180°C). Season the duck with salt and pepper inside and out. In a casserole dish suitable for the oven, heat the extra virgin olive oil over medium-high heat. Sear the duck for about 10-12 minutes, turning it on all sides until the skin becomes golden and crispy. This step develops deeper flavors and enhances the overall texture, making the skin crispy. Transfer the duck to a plate and set aside.

2. **Prepare the Sauce Base:** In the same casserole dish, add the chopped onion and sauté for about 5 minutes until softened and translucent. The onion will create a sweet and flavorful base for the sauce. Add the minced garlic and cook for another 2 minutes, being careful not to let it burn. Add the prunes and cook for another 2 minutes, stirring well to blend the flavors. This step allows the prunes to soften and balance the acidity of the sauce with their sweetness.

3. **Add the Liquids and Flavorings:** Pour the red wine into the casserole to deglaze, incorporating all the browned bits from the bottom. Let it cook for 5 minutes until the alcohol evaporates, intensifying the flavor without overpowering it. Then add the chicken broth, red wine vinegar, cinnamon, honey, thyme sprig, and orange zest. Stir well and bring to a boil. The cinnamon adds a warm, spiced note, while the orange zest provides a touch of freshness that balances the richness of the sauce.

4. **Bake in the Oven:** Return the duck to the casserole, partially immersing it in the sauce. Cover the casserole with a lid or aluminum foil and transfer to the preheated oven. Cook for about 1 hour and 15 minutes, basting the duck with the sauce every 20-30 minutes to keep it moist and flavorful. The meat should be tender, and the sauce thick and aromatic.

5. **Assemble and Serve:** Remove the duck from the casserole and let it rest for a few minutes before cutting it into pieces. If the sauce is too thin, reduce it over medium heat on the stove for a few minutes until you reach the desired consistency. Arrange the duck pieces on a serving platter and pour the prune sauce over them. Garnish with fresh chopped parsley and serve immediately. This dish pairs well with mashed potatoes or roasted seasonal vegetables, which absorb the rich and flavorful sauce. For a finishing touch, add a few fresh orange slices to enhance the visual appeal and contrast of flavors.

6. **Variations and Suggestions:**

- **Fruit Substitution**: If preferred, you can replace the prunes with dried figs or dried apricots to vary the flavor of the sauce. Figs add a sweet and slightly earthy note, while apricots provide a pleasant acidity that pairs well with the red wine.
- **Spiced Variation**: Add a pinch of ground cloves or a dash of allspice for an even more complex and spiced flavor.
- **Side Pairings**: This dish goes perfectly with a side of basmati rice or creamy polenta. Another option could be a fresh spinach salad with toasted walnuts and a light lemon dressing, or garnishing with fresh thyme or rosemary sprigs for a crunchy, refreshing, and aromatic component that contrasts with the richness of the duck and sauce.

Side Dishes

Introduction: Origins and Reinterpretation of Medieval Side Dishes

Medieval side dishes, while often seen as just an accompaniment to main courses, played a fundamental role in the daily diets of both the noble and common classes. During the Middle Ages, the seasonal availability of ingredients and the social and economic differences deeply influenced the preparation and variety of side dishes. For instance, sides made from cabbages and legumes were typical among the poorer classes during winter, while the noble courts might enjoy dishes like braised leeks with exotic spices, symbolizing prestige and wealth. Among the poorer classes, cabbages, turnips, and beans were common winter foods, whereas the nobility could afford more exquisite vegetables and expensive spices throughout the year. The differences in side dishes consumed by the nobles and those by the less affluent clearly mirrored the limited or abundant access to certain ingredients and resources. For example, in noble courts, vegetables might be enhanced with rare spices like saffron, which was extremely costly and displayed the host's prestige, while among the common folk, ordinary vegetables were simply boiled with local herbs to enhance the flavor.

In medieval courts, side dishes were prepared with care and complexity, using elaborate cooking techniques such as braising, baking, and slow stewing, as in the case of leeks braised with precious spices, which were seen as symbols of prestige. Vegetables like chard, leeks, carrots, and cabbages were flavored with valuable spices such as pepper, nutmeg, and cloves—all imported from distant lands and considered symbols of prestige. The combination of vegetables and dried fruits, like plums and raisins, helped create an interesting balance of sweet and savory flavors, highly appreciated in the medieval cuisine of the upper classes for the unique contrast between sweetness and acidity, reflecting the taste for complexity typical of the era. The use of honey and vinegar to prepare sweet and sour dishes was particularly widespread, giving the vegetables a rich and complex taste. This balance of flavors was not just a matter of taste but also represented the culinary sophistication of the time, often used to impress guests during noble banquets and festivities.

For the peasants and common folk, side dishes were much simpler and based on locally available and seasonal ingredients. The dishes mainly consisted of legumes, roots, and wild vegetables like nettles and dandelions, which were often boiled or used in stews. These sides were essential for providing plant proteins and fiber, and the use of aromatic herbs such as thyme, sage, and parsley helped enhance the flavor of the dishes, making them more palatable despite their simplicity. Peasant cooking was infused with practicality, and nothing was wasted: every part of the vegetables and herbs was used to enrich the meal. For example, carrot leaves, often discarded, were used to prepare aromatic broths or added to simple soups.

The modern reinterpretation of medieval side dishes strives to maintain the historical essence of these dishes, adapting them to contemporary tastes and culinary techniques, while making them more accessible and suitable for modern nutritional needs. Today, vegetables like carrots, cauliflowers, and turnips can be roasted in the oven with spices to maintain their authentic flavor but with a crunchier texture and a more refined presentation. The use of dried fruits and honey to balance flavors remains a key element, enriched, however, by modern cooking techniques like sous-vide cooking, which allows for preserving the nutrients and texture of the ingredients. For example, carrots cooked sous-vide and then briefly roasted can offer an incredibly tender texture while retaining all the natural flavor.

This section of the book dedicated to reinterpreted medieval side dishes includes a variety of recipes, such as braised chard with spices or boiled nettles, ranging from the simplest dishes inspired by peasant cooking to the more elaborate sides typical of noble tables. The goal is to rediscover and enhance ancient flavors using seasonal ingredients and traditional techniques, but with a touch of modernity that makes them perfect for today's palates. For instance, vegetables can be roasted to enhance their natural sweetness or cooked sous-vide to keep their nutrients intact, thus creating a taste experience that blends tradition and innovation. The addition of sides like parsnip puree with honey or braised vegetables with exotic spices allows for the re-presentation of the charm of medieval cuisine in a modern key, capable of surprising and delighting. Among the recipes offered, you can also find dishes like honey-glazed carrots with spices or leeks braised in white wine, which pay homage to the medieval tradition but with a contemporary twist that enhances the quality of the ingredients.

Roasted Vegetables with Honey and Spices

This medieval-inspired recipe has its roots in the culinary traditions of European courts, particularly those of the Valois in France and the Medici in Italy, where precious spices like cinnamon and honey symbolized wealth and prestige. Vegetables were often prepared with sweet and spicy flavors, reflecting the era's passion for complex and refined tastes.

Preparation Time: 20 minutes

Total Time: 1 hour

Servings: 4

Ingredients:

- 2 large carrots, sliced into rounds
- 2 parsnips, cut into sticks
- 1 red onion, cut into wedges
- 1 zucchini, sliced into rounds
- 2 tablespoons extra virgin olive oil
- 2 tablespoons honey
- 1 teaspoon ground cinnamon
- 1/2 teaspoon ground cloves
- 1/2 teaspoon nutmeg
- Salt and pepper to taste
- Fresh parsley, chopped, for garnish

Instructions:

1. **Preparing the Vegetables:** Preheat the oven to 400°F (200°C). Prepare all the vegetables by cutting them as indicated to ensure even cooking. Take your time to slice the vegetables uniformly, as this will help them cook evenly and achieve the desired texture. Arrange the vegetables in a single layer on a large baking sheet to ensure proper caramelization and prevent steaming, which would make them soggy. It is important to use a baking sheet that is large enough to allow space between the vegetables, as overcrowding will lead to uneven cooking and a less desirable texture.

2. **Seasoning the Vegetables:** In a bowl, mix the extra virgin olive oil, honey, cinnamon, cloves, nutmeg, salt, and pepper. This seasoning reinterprets medieval flavors by combining sweetness and aromatic spices like honey, cinnamon, and cloves, typical of the era, for a harmonious and rich balance. The honey provides a natural sweetness, while the spices contribute warmth and depth, making this dish truly evocative of medieval culinary traditions. Pour the seasoning over the vegetables and mix well to ensure they are evenly coated. Take a moment to massage the seasoning into the vegetables, ensuring that each piece is thoroughly covered for maximum flavor.

3. **Roasting:** Place the baking sheet in the preheated oven and roast the vegetables for about 40 minutes, stirring halfway through to ensure even browning. The vegetables should be tender with caramelized, golden edges, giving off a fragrant, spiced aroma that fills the kitchen. The roasting process brings out the natural sugars in the vegetables, enhancing their sweetness and creating a beautiful contrast with the warm spices. Be sure to check the vegetables periodically to avoid overcooking, as the goal is to achieve a tender yet slightly crisp texture with caramelized edges. Stirring the vegetables halfway through the cooking process helps to ensure that they brown evenly and do not stick to the baking sheet.

4. **Assembly and Serving:** Once cooked, remove the vegetables from the oven and transfer them to a serving platter. Garnish with chopped fresh parsley to add a touch of color and freshness to the dish. The bright green parsley not only enhances the visual appeal but also adds a fresh, slightly peppery note that complements the sweetness of the roasted vegetables. Serve immediately as a side for meat or fish dishes, or as a vegetarian main course accompanied by rustic bread. The bread can be used to soak up any remaining honey and spice glaze, making every bite full of flavor.

5. **Variations and Tips:**
   - **Alternative Vegetables:** You can substitute the vegetables with seasonal options like squash, sweet potatoes, or beets to adapt the dish to seasonal availability. Squash, for example, adds a natural sweetness that pairs perfectly with honey and spices.
   - **Spicier Flavor:** Add a pinch of cayenne pepper for a touch of heat that contrasts with the sweetness of the honey.

- **Pairings:** This dish pairs well with roasted meats or poultry, but can also be served over a bed of couscous for a complete meal. Alternatively, serve it with grilled tofu for a vegetarian option.
- **Versatility:** The caramelized honey and aromatic spices make this a versatile side dish suitable for many pairings, such as pork roasts, baked duck, or grilled fish, which benefit from the sweetness and spiced notes of this dish.

Chickpea Pottage with Aromatic Herbs

This chickpea pottage is a rustic dish rooted in the medieval European culinary tradition, particularly in the rural regions of Central Italy, Southern France, and Spain, where legumes and local herbs were fundamental ingredients for creating hearty and nutritious meals. Popular among rural communities, pottage was made to make the best use of available resources, turning a few simple ingredients into a flavorful and comforting meal.

Preparation Time: 15 minutes

Total Time: 1 hour 15 minutes

Servings: 4

Ingredients:

- 10.5 oz (300 g) dried chickpeas (soaked for at least 8 hours)
- 2 tablespoons extra virgin olive oil
- 1 large onion, chopped
- 2 cloves garlic, minced
- 2 carrots, sliced into rounds
- 1 celery stalk, chopped
- 1 bay leaf
- 1 sprig fresh rosemary
- 1 teaspoon dried thyme
- 1 tablespoon fresh parsley, chopped

- 4 cups (1 liter) vegetable broth
- Salt and pepper to taste

Instructions:

1. **Preparing the Chickpeas:** Rinse the soaked chickpeas under running water and drain well. This step helps remove any impurities and improves their digestibility, reducing the complex sugars that can cause digestive discomfort. In a large pot, heat the extra virgin olive oil over medium heat. The soaking process is crucial, as it helps to soften the chickpeas, making them easier to cook and more pleasant to eat.

2. **Vegetable Sauté:** Add the chopped onion and sauté for about 5 minutes, until soft and translucent. The onion serves as the base of the dish, providing a sweet and savory depth. Add the garlic, carrots, and celery, and continue to cook for another 5 minutes, stirring frequently. The garlic adds a rich, aromatic flavor that complements the sweetness of the carrots and the earthy notes of the celery. This sauté is essential for creating a rich and deep aromatic base, layering flavors and enhancing the complexity of the dish. Taking the time to properly sauté the vegetables ensures that the final dish will have a well-developed taste.

3. **Adding Chickpeas and Herbs:** Add the drained chickpeas to the pot along with the bay leaf and rosemary sprig. Stir well to combine the ingredients and let cook for 5-10 minutes, allowing the chickpeas and herbs to fully develop their flavors. The aromatic herbs give the pottage a rustic and authentic character, typical of traditional cooking, where these herbs were commonly used for their availability and their ability to enhance simple dishes. The bay leaf and rosemary infuse the chickpeas with a subtle, woodsy aroma that deepens the flavor profile of the dish, making it hearty and satisfying.

4. **Cooking the Pottage:** Pour the vegetable broth into the pot and bring to a boil. Reduce the heat, cover, and let simmer for about 1 hour, or until the chickpeas are tender and the consistency is creamy. If needed, add a bit of water during cooking to prevent the pottage from drying out. Slow cooking allows the flavors to develop and meld together, creating a rich and comforting dish. The gentle simmering also ensures that the chickpeas become tender without losing their shape, resulting in a perfect texture. The broth gradually thickens as it cooks, enveloping the chickpeas and vegetables in a flavorful, creamy base that is both hearty and warming.

5. **Finishing and Serving:** Remove the bay leaf and rosemary sprig from the pot. Adjust the seasoning with salt and pepper, then add the dried thyme and chopped fresh parsley. Stir well and let cook for another 5 minutes to blend the final flavors. The thyme and parsley add a fresh, herbal note that brightens the dish and balances the richness of the chickpeas. Serve the pottage hot, accompanied by rustic bread or croutons for a complete and nutritious meal. The bread serves as the perfect accompaniment, allowing you to soak up every bit of the flavorful broth. For an extra touch, you can drizzle a bit of extra

virgin olive oil over the top before serving, adding a silky texture and enhancing the overall taste.

6. **Variations and Suggestions:**
   - **Fruit Substitution:** If preferred, you can replace the chickpeas with white beans or lentils to vary the flavor and texture of the pottage. Lentils require less cooking time, making the dish quicker to prepare.
   - **Spiced Variation:** Try adding sage or marjoram for a different touch and a more complex aromatic profile. These herbs pair well with chickpeas and further enrich the dish.
   - **Side Pairings:** This pottage pairs perfectly with whole-grain bread or herb focaccia. Another option could be a fresh spinach salad with toasted walnuts and a light lemon dressing, or garnishing with fresh thyme or rosemary sprigs for a crunchy, refreshing, and aromatic component that contrasts with the richness of the pottage. You can also serve it with a drizzle of extra virgin olive oil to enhance the flavors and add a note of freshness.

Turnip and Goat Cheese Puree

This simple and delicious dish has medieval origins, particularly in the rural regions of Central and Southern Europe, such as present-day Italy and Spain, where turnips were a staple food for agricultural communities. During the Middle Ages, turnip puree was often prepared as a side dish, providing an economical and nutritious option in peasant kitchens. The addition of goat cheese made the turnip puree a more nutritious and versatile preparation, capable of enhancing local resources and adapting to the needs of everyday life.

Preparation Time: 20 minutes

Total Time: 40 minutes

Servings: 4

Ingredients:

- lb (500 g) turnips, peeled and cut into pieces
- 1/2 cup (100 ml) whole milk
- 1.8 oz (50 g) butter
- 3.5 oz (100 g) fresh goat cheese
- Salt and pepper to taste
- 1 tablespoon fresh parsley, chopped, for garnish

Instructions:

1   **Preparing the Turnips:** Bring a pot of lightly salted water to a boil. Add the peeled and cut turnips and cook for about 20 minutes, or until they are soft enough to be easily mashed with a fork. The turnips should be tender enough that a fork pierces them without difficulty. Drain well and transfer them to a large bowl.

2   **Making the Puree:** In a small saucepan, heat the milk and butter over medium heat until the butter is completely melted and the milk is hot, but not boiling. It is important not to boil the milk to avoid altering the consistency of the puree or negatively affecting the flavor. This step ensures that the puree is creamy and smooth. Add the heated milk and butter to the cooked turnips and begin mashing them with a potato masher or an immersion blender until you achieve a smooth and velvety consistency. For a smoother texture, it is recommended to use an immersion blender, while a potato masher will give a more rustic texture.

3   **Adding the Goat Cheese:** Add the fresh goat cheese to the puree while the mixture is still warm, but off the heat, and stir until fully incorporated. The goat cheese adds a rich and slightly tangy flavor to the puree, balancing the sweetness of the turnips and adding creaminess that enhances the texture of the dish. Season with salt and pepper to taste, ensuring the flavors are well balanced.

4   **Assembling and Serving:** Transfer the puree to a serving dish and garnish with chopped fresh parsley to add a touch of color and freshness. Serve the turnip puree hot as a side dish for roasted meats or fish fillets, such as baked sea bass or cod. Alternatively, it can be part of a vegetarian meal, accompanied by rustic bread or grilled vegetables for a more complete and balanced option.

5   **Variations and Suggestions:**
   - **Dairy-Free Version:** If you prefer a dairy-free version, you can substitute the milk with unsweetened almond milk and the butter with extra virgin olive oil. This version will maintain the creaminess of the puree without using animal products.
   - **Cheese Substitutes:** You can replace the goat cheese with sheep's cheese for a milder flavor, or with blue cheese for a more intense and distinctive note.
   - **Pairings:** This puree pairs perfectly with roasted meats, such as lamb or pork, but it can also be served with baked fish fillets. For a more elegant presentation, garnish the dish with a few thin slices of raw turnip marinated in white wine vinegar for about 15-20 minutes, adding a pleasant contrast of textures.

Desserts

Introduction: Origins and Reinterpretation of Medieval Desserts

Medieval desserts, often reserved for special occasions and noble tables, were considered a luxury in an era when sugar, primarily imported from distant lands like India and the Middle East, was deemed a rare and costly spice. The challenges of transportation and the scarce availability in Europe made these ingredients highly prized. Most confections were sweetened with honey, which served dual purposes as both a sweetener and a preservative. Ingredients like dried fruits, precious spices, and fresh fruits were commonly used to enhance flavors and signify wealth and abundance. Spices such as cinnamon, cloves, pepper, and ginger added an exotic flair that emphasized the status of affluent families capable of acquiring them. Moreover, dried fruits like almonds, walnuts, and dates not only enhanced the flavors but were also imbued with symbolic meanings associated with fertility and prosperity.

In the medieval era, desserts played a crucial role not just in feasts and celebrations but also as potent religious and social symbols. Many sweets were specially prepared for religious festivities such as Christmas and Easter or to mark significant life events like weddings and births. Dessert making was an intricate art typically reserved for skilled court chefs or monks, who had access to rare ingredients and the expertise needed to craft elaborate and symbolically rich treats. For instance, 'spice biscuits,' typically prepared during Christmas, were loaded with luxurious ingredients like spices and honey. 'Almond sweets' were often featured at wedding feasts to symbolize the union and prosperity of the newlyweds. In many monastic communities, monks engaged in making desserts like 'panforte,' a dense cake filled with dried fruits and spices, symbolizing the generosity and virtue of monastic life. Even pilgrims were often given simple sweets as a sign of hospitality, highlighting the charitable aspect of desserts in medieval culture.

Today's reinterpretation of medieval desserts strives to preserve the historical essence of these delicacies while adapting them to contemporary tastes and dietary needs. The use of refined sugar, honey alternatives, and more accessible spices makes these desserts easier to prepare, while modern culinary techniques like convection baking, and the use of mixers and blenders for dough preparation, enhance their texture and presentation. Fruit tarts, once made with dried fruits and honey, typical of the era, are now reimagined with fresh fruits and a lighter pastry base, offering a more refined texture and a fresher taste than their historical counterparts. Similarly, spiced cakes, which were once dense and rustic, are now enriched with modern ingredients like cream and butter to achieve a softer and more appealing texture. Modern culinary techniques, such as the use of egg white foams and contemporary leavening agents, help produce lighter desserts that align with today's preference for fluffier and airier textures.

In this expanded section dedicated to reimagined medieval desserts, we delve into a variety of recipes that draw inspiration from tradition but are tailored to suit modern palates. Each recipe is designed to maintain a connection to its historical roots while celebrating the rich flavors and ingredients typical of the time, yet ensuring they are appropriate for contemporary dining tables. This approach respects traditional tastes but modifies the richness and sweetness to better align with modern preferences. Whether featuring spiced biscuits, almond cakes, or honey-based sweets, these dishes bring with them the history and elegance of a bygone era, creatively reinterpreted with respect for tradition. Additionally, the recipes include suggestions for modern presentations, such as garnishing with fresh fruits and edible flowers, to make these desserts visually appealing for today's discerning diners. This reinterpretation of medieval desserts not only revives the authentic flavors of the past but also presents them in an aesthetically pleasing and contextually appropriate manner for every special occasion, from casual family meals to more formal dinners.

Blancmanger

Blancmanger has ancient origins dating back to the Middle Ages, when it was prepared as a symbol of refinement for the nobility. This recipe likely originated in France and then spread throughout Europe due to cultural influences of medieval courts. Originally, it was made with white meat, rice, and almond milk, combining sweet and savory flavors typical of the cuisines of the time.

Preparation Time: 30 minutes

Total Time: 1 hour 30 minutes

Servings: 6

Ingredients:

- 2 cups (500 ml) unsweetened almond milk
- 1/2 cup (100 g) rice
- 3/4 cup (150 g) sugar
- oz (200 g) cooked and shredded chicken breast (optional)
- 1 teaspoon rose water
- 1 teaspoon ground cinnamon
- 1.8 oz (50 g) chopped almonds
- Salt to taste
- Fresh parsley for garnish (optional)

Instructions:

1. **Preparing the Rice:** In a medium-sized saucepan, bring the almond milk to a gentle boil with a pinch of salt. Almond milk was highly prized in medieval cuisine for its unique flavor and versatility, often used as a substitute for dairy in both savory and sweet dishes. Once the milk is boiling, add the rice and reduce the heat to low. Let it simmer for about 30-35 minutes, stirring occasionally to prevent sticking, until the rice is soft and has absorbed almost all the milk. The rice should be tender enough to be easily mashed with a fork without resistance. This step requires patience to ensure the rice does not stick to the bottom of the pan and to achieve a creamy, smooth consistency. Stirring also helps create an even texture throughout, contributing to the luxurious feel of the final dish.

2. **Adding the Aromatic Ingredients:** Once the rice has reached the desired consistency, add the sugar and stir well to dissolve completely. The sweetness of the sugar balances the savory undertones of the almond milk and rice, creating a harmonious blend of flavors. If you want to follow the original medieval blancmanger recipe, add the shredded chicken breast to the rice at this stage. The addition of chicken contributes to the historical authenticity of the dish and provides an intriguing balance between sweet and savory, which was a hallmark of medieval cooking. Stir the chicken until it is well incorporated, and let the mixture cook for another 10 minutes, allowing the flavors to meld together. The use of chicken, though unusual for a modern dessert, adds a depth of flavor that is both unique and reflective of medieval tastes, offering a glimpse into the culinary traditions of the past.

3. **Flavoring with Rose Water and Cinnamon:** Remove the saucepan from the heat and add the rose water and ground cinnamon. Rose water was widely used in medieval cooking, especially in dishes meant for the nobility, as it provided an exotic and aromatic quality. The rose water gives the blancmanger a delicate floral aroma that complements the sweetness of the rice and sugar. The amount of rose water can be adjusted to taste, as its flavor can be quite intense for some people—it's best to start with a small amount and add more if desired. Stir well to distribute the flavors evenly, ensuring that the floral and spicy notes are balanced throughout the mixture. The addition of cinnamon adds warmth and complexity, further enhancing the dish's medieval character.

4. **Assembling and Cooling:** Pour the mixture into small, lightly oiled molds or a large serving bowl and allow it to cool to room temperature. Lightly oiling the molds helps the blancmanger release easily once set. Once cooled, cover and transfer the molds to the refrigerator for at least 30 minutes, or until the blancmanger is set. The cooling process allows the flavors to intensify and the dessert to firm up, resulting in a texture that is both creamy and slightly gelatinous. This step is crucial for achieving the characteristic consistency of blancmanger, which should be firm enough to hold its shape but soft enough to melt in the mouth.

5. **Garnishing and Serving:** Before serving, garnish the blancmanger with chopped almonds, preferably toasted beforehand to enhance their flavor and add a crunchy texture that contrasts with the smoothness of the dessert. The toasted almonds also bring out the nutty

flavor of the almond milk, creating a cohesive taste experience. If desired, you can add a few sprigs of fresh parsley for decoration—this was a common practice in medieval times, where even desserts were often garnished with herbs for visual appeal and added freshness. Serve the blancmanger cold as a delicate and aromatic dessert, perfect for concluding a meal in a refined way. The combination of floral, sweet, and nutty flavors makes it an elegant choice for special occasions or dinner parties.

6   **Variations and Suggestions:**

- **Vegetarian Version:** You can omit the chicken for a completely vegetarian version of blancmanger, which will be more like a modern rice pudding but with the characteristic floral aroma of rose water.

- **Milk Substitutes:** If preferred, you can use coconut milk or cow's milk for a different version of the dish. Coconut milk will add an exotic note, while cow's milk will give a milder flavor.

- **Spice Variations:** For a more complex flavor, you can add a pinch of nutmeg or ginger along with the cinnamon. These spices were widely used in medieval cooking and further enrich the aromatic profile of the dessert.

Almond and Honey Cake

The Almond and Honey Cake has ancient roots in medieval culinary tradition, when honey was the primary sweetener, long before sugar became a common ingredient. This simple yet rich dessert was a symbol of celebration in noble courts, where almonds and spices were considered prestigious ingredients. The recipe likely originated in the Mediterranean regions, particularly in Italy and Spain, where almonds were abundantly cultivated.

Preparation Time: 20 minutes

Total Time: 1 hour 10 minutes

Servings: 8

Ingredients:

- oz (200 g) chopped almonds
- oz (150 g) almond flour
- oz (150 g) honey
- 3.5 oz (100 g) butter
- 3 eggs
- 1 teaspoon ground cinnamon
- 1/2 teaspoon nutmeg
- Grated zest of 1 lemon
- 1 teaspoon vanilla extract
- Pinch of salt

- Whole almonds for decoration

Instructions:

1. **Preparing the Batter**: Preheat the oven to 350°F (180°C) and grease a round cake pan with butter or line it with parchment paper. In a large bowl, beat the softened butter with the honey until the mixture is creamy and smooth. The combination of butter and honey should be light and fluffy, which will help create a tender crumb once baked. Add the eggs one at a time, making sure they are at room temperature, mixing well after each addition to fully incorporate them. Room temperature eggs ensure that the batter emulsifies properly, giving the cake a soft and even texture. This helps create a light and airy batter that will give the cake its soft texture.

2. **Adding the Dry Ingredients**: In another bowl, mix the almond flour, chopped almonds, cinnamon, nutmeg, lemon zest, and pinch of salt. These dry ingredients will give the cake a rich texture and a spiced aroma reminiscent of medieval flavors. The lemon zest adds a fresh, citrusy note that cuts through the richness, while the spices bring warmth and complexity. Gradually add the dry ingredients to the butter, honey, and egg mixture, folding gently until well combined. Be careful not to overmix, as this can lead to a denser cake. Finally, add the vanilla extract to complete the aromatic profile of the cake. The vanilla enhances the natural sweetness and balances the spices, giving the cake a well-rounded flavor.

3. **Baking the Cake**: Pour the batter into the prepared cake pan and level the surface with a spatula. The smooth surface will ensure even baking and a visually appealing result. Arrange the whole almonds on top for decoration, pressing them slightly into the batter. This not only adds visual appeal but also provides a delightful crunch in each bite. Bake the cake in the preheated oven for about 40-45 minutes, or until a toothpick inserted into the center comes out clean. If using a convection oven, check a few minutes earlier, as it may bake more quickly. The cake should be golden on the surface and soft inside, with a slight spring when touched, indicating that it is perfectly baked.

4. **Cooling and Serving**: Once baked, let the cake cool in the pan for 10 minutes to allow it to set, reducing the risk of breaking when transferred. Cooling in the pan initially helps the cake stabilize and prevents it from falling apart when handled. Then transfer it to a wire rack to cool completely. Cooling helps develop the flavors and stabilize the texture, ensuring that each slice is moist and tender. Serve the cake at room temperature, drizzled with extra honey to enhance the natural sweetness of the dessert. The added honey creates a beautiful glaze and intensifies the cake's richness, making it even more indulgent. For an added touch, you can sprinkle a bit of cinnamon on top of the honey drizzle to enhance the warm flavors.

5. **Variations and Suggestions:**

- **Alternative Honey:** You can experiment with different types of honey, such as chestnut or acacia honey, to vary the flavor of the cake. Chestnut honey, for example, will add a more intense and slightly bitter note, while acacia honey will make the cake more delicate. To further enrich the cake, you can add raisins or chopped dried figs to the batter. These ingredients were often used in medieval times to add sweetness and texture to desserts.
- **Pairings:** This cake pairs perfectly with a cup of herbal tea or spiced infusion, for a tasting experience that evokes the atmosphere of medieval courts. The warm spices and the natural sweetness of the honey make it an ideal companion for a relaxing afternoon or an elegant ending to a meal.

Medieval Spiced Cookies

Medieval Spiced Cookies have their origins in the Middle Ages and were made as a special treat for festive occasions, particularly during religious holidays. These cookies were rich in spices such as cinnamon, ginger, and cloves—ingredients that were expensive and rare at the time, whose use denoted wealth and prestige. The recipe likely originated in Northern Europe, where exotic spices were imported by merchants via trade routes, and spread throughout the continent thanks to cultural exchanges among medieval courts.

Preparation Time: 20 minutes

Total Time: 1 hour

Servings: 20 cookies

Ingredients:

- oz (200 g) all-purpose flour
- 3.5 oz (100 g) butter
- 3.5 oz (100 g) honey
- 1.8 oz (50 g) brown sugar
- 1 egg
- 1 teaspoon ground cinnamon
- 1/2 teaspoon ground ginger
- 1/2 teaspoon ground cloves
- 1/2 teaspoon nutmeg

- Pinch of salt
- Grated zest of 1 orange

Instructions:

1 **Preparing the Dry Ingredients**: In a large bowl, sift the flour and add the cinnamon, ginger, cloves, nutmeg, and salt. Mix well to distribute the spices evenly throughout the flour. These spices were widely used in medieval cuisine for their intense aroma and the symbolic value associated with wealth and their exotic origins. They were often imported through trade routes such as the Spice Route, which connected Asia to Europe, bringing a wide range of flavors that added depth to medieval cooking. Their use denoted prestige and access to luxury goods, making these ingredients symbols of power and social status.

2 **Mixing the Wet Ingredients**: In another bowl, beat the softened butter with the brown sugar until creamy and smooth. The creamed butter and sugar should have a light, fluffy consistency, as this will help the cookies achieve a tender texture. Add the honey and egg, mixing well to incorporate all the ingredients. Honey, in addition to sweetening, gives the cookies a soft texture and a rich, complex flavor that is characteristic of medieval recipes. Honey was preferred over sugar in many medieval dishes, as it was more readily available and had preservative qualities, making it a versatile and valuable ingredient in cooking. It also added a floral undertone that complemented the warmth of the spices.

3 **Forming the Dough**: Gradually add the dry ingredient mixture to the wet ingredients, mixing until a homogeneous dough forms. Be sure to add the dry ingredients slowly to avoid lumps and to ensure even distribution of the spices throughout the dough. Add the grated orange zest to give a touch of freshness that balances the complexity of the spices. The orange zest not only adds a citrusy note but also enhances the overall flavor, making the cookies more aromatic and vibrant. Wrap the dough in plastic wrap and let it rest in the refrigerator for at least 30 minutes. This step helps firm up the dough, making it easier to work with and enhancing the flavors by allowing the spices to infuse the dough. Chilling the dough also ensures that the cookies maintain their shape during baking.

4 **Shaping and Baking the Cookies**: Preheat the oven to 350°F (180°C). On a lightly floured surface, roll out the dough to about 1/4 inch (5 mm) thickness. Use round or traditional cookie cutters to cut out the cookies. You can also use cutters shaped like stars, hearts, or other festive symbols to make the cookies even more special. Place them on a baking sheet lined with parchment paper, leaving a little space between each cookie to allow for slight spreading during baking. Bake the cookies in the preheated oven for about 12-15 minutes, or until the edges are lightly golden. The aroma of the spices will fill the kitchen, creating a warm and inviting atmosphere reminiscent of medieval festivities. Watch the cookies closely in the last few minutes of baking to ensure they do not overbake, as the edges can brown quickly.

5   **Cooling and Serving**: Once baked, let the cookies cool on the baking sheet for 5 minutes to allow them to set before transferring. Then, transfer them to a wire rack to cool completely. Cooling allows the cookies to become crisp and develop their full spiced flavor. It is important to cool the cookies on a rack to prevent excess moisture from making them soft on the bottom. The cooling process also allows the flavors to mature, making the cookies even more flavorful. Serve the cookies with a cup of spiced tea or warm mulled wine for an experience that evokes the festive atmosphere of medieval times. These cookies are perfect for sharing during winter holidays or as part of a medieval-themed gathering.

6   **Variations and Suggestions:**
   - **Additions:** You can add raisins or chopped dried fruit to the dough to further enrich the cookies. Raisins, for example, add natural sweetness that pairs well with the spices.
   - **Decorative Glaze:** For a more decorative version, you can prepare a glaze with powdered sugar and a pinch of cinnamon to brush onto the cookies once cooled. This detail not only adds sweetness but also makes the cookies more visually appealing.
   - **Pairings:** These cookies pair perfectly with a glass of spiced wine or strong black tea, which enhance the aromatic notes of the spices, making them an ideal choice for a cozy and festive treat.

Fried Egg Raviolo

The Fried Egg Raviolo has medieval origins, when dishes enriched with eggs and cheese were considered symbols of abundance and prestige. This recipe, which likely originated in the central regions of Italy, was prepared during festive occasions and represented a true delicacy due to the use of fresh and valuable ingredients like butter and spices.

Preparation Time: 25 minutes

Total Time: 45 minutes

Servings: 4 ravioli (1 per serving)

Ingredients:

- oz (200 g) all-purpose flour
- eggs (2 for the dough and 1 for each raviolo filling)
- 1.8 oz (50 g) butter
- 1.8 oz (50 g) fresh cheese (such as ricotta or mascarpone)
- 1 teaspoon sugar
- Pinch of salt
- Oil for frying
- 1 teaspoon ground cinnamon
- Honey for garnish

Instructions:

1 **Preparing the Dough**: In a large bowl, sift the flour and add a pinch of salt and the sugar. Make a well in the center and add two room-temperature eggs. Using a fork, begin incorporating the flour from the sides towards the center until a homogeneous dough forms. Transfer the dough to a lightly floured surface and knead for about 10 minutes, until smooth and elastic. This kneading process is essential to develop the gluten in the flour, which will give the ravioli its desired texture. Wrap the dough in plastic wrap and let it rest for at least 15 minutes. Resting the dough allows the gluten to relax, making it easier to roll out and work with later.

2 **Preparing the Filling**: In a small bowl, mix the fresh cheese with a bit of ground cinnamon for an aromatic touch. The cinnamon adds a warm, slightly sweet note that complements the richness of the cheese. Roll out the dough with a rolling pin until it is a thin sheet, about 2-3 mm thick. Cut the dough into squares of about 4 inches (10 cm) per side. Place a small amount of cheese in the center of each square and create a small well, where you will carefully crack an egg yolk. Be careful during this step to avoid breaking the yolk prematurely, as this may make it difficult to close the raviolo. The combination of the cheese and egg yolk creates a luscious, creamy filling that contrasts beautifully with the crispy exterior.

3 **Sealing and Frying the Ravioli**: Close the raviolo by placing another square of dough on top, pressing firmly along the edges to seal, ensuring that any air inside is pushed out to prevent the raviolo from opening during frying. To ensure a perfect seal, you can use a fork to crimp the edges or press them tightly with your fingers. Make sure to seal carefully around the yolk to avoid leakage during cooking. Heat the oil in a deep skillet until it reaches about 340°F (170°C). It is important to use enough oil to fully submerge the ravioli for even cooking. Fry the ravioli, one at a time, for about 2-3 minutes, until they are golden and crispy, turning them gently for even cooking. Frying one at a time helps maintain a consistent oil temperature, which is key to achieving a crispy texture without making the ravioli too greasy. The sizzling sound and the aroma of the frying ravioli add to the sensory experience, making the cooking process just as enjoyable as eating the finished dish.

4 **Cooling and Serving**: Drain the ravioli on paper towels to remove excess oil. This helps keep the exterior crisp and prevents the dish from becoming too oily. Serve them hot, garnished with a drizzle of honey, a sprinkle of ground cinnamon, or alternatively with powdered sugar or a light drizzle of caramel for added variety. The honey provides a floral sweetness that pairs wonderfully with the richness of the fried dough and the creamy filling. Serving immediately helps preserve the contrast between the crispy exterior and the soft interior. The contrast between the creamy, soft filling and the crisp shell makes this dish a true delight, ideal to serve as a dessert during a special dinner. The combination of textures and flavors—crispy, creamy, sweet, and spiced—offers a unique culinary experience that is both decadent and comforting.

5 **Variations and Suggestions:**

- **Sweeter Version:** For a sweeter version, you can add a bit of sugar to the cheese and enrich the filling with raisins or grated lemon zest. This will give the raviolo a more complex and aromatic flavor.

- **Baked Version:** If you prefer a lighter version, you can bake the ravioli in a preheated oven at 350°F (180°C) for about 20 minutes, until golden. This alternative keeps the crispness while reducing the use of oil.

- **Pairings:** These ravioli pair well with a glass of dessert wine, such as Vin Santo, which enhances the aromatic notes of the cinnamon and honey. Alternatively, you can serve them with spiced tea or an herbal infusion for a non-alcoholic option.

Fig and Walnut Fritters

Fig and Walnut Fritters are a traditional medieval dessert, created to celebrate the abundance of autumn fruits. Figs, considered precious for their nutritional properties, and walnuts, symbols of prosperity, were often used together to create simple yet flavorful sweets. This recipe has its roots in the rural areas of central Italy, where these ingredients were available during the seasonal harvest.

Preparation Time: 20 minutes

Total Time: 40 minutes

Servings: 10 fritters

Ingredients:

- oz (200 g) dried figs
- 3.5 oz (100 g) coarsely chopped walnuts
- oz (150 g) all-purpose flour
- 2 eggs
- 1.8 oz (50 g) brown sugar
- 3.4 fl oz (100 ml) milk
- 1 teaspoon ground cinnamon
- Pinch of salt
- Oil for frying
- Honey for garnish

Instructions:

1. **Preparing the Batter:** Cut the dried figs into small pieces and set them aside. In a large bowl, sift the flour and add the salt and cinnamon. Sifting the flour is important to remove any lumps and aerate the mixture, resulting in a lighter texture. In another bowl, beat the eggs with the brown sugar until the mixture becomes frothy. Gradually add the milk while continuing to mix, then slowly incorporate the flour until a smooth, lump-free batter forms. The consistency should be thick but pourable.

2. **Adding the Figs and Walnuts:** Add the chopped dried figs and walnuts to the batter, mixing well to distribute the ingredients evenly. Ensure that each spoonful of batter contains a good amount of figs and walnuts to guarantee a balanced flavor in every fritter. The combination of figs and walnuts provides a delightful blend of sweetness and nuttiness, making each bite rich in texture and taste.

3. **Frying the Fritters:** Heat the oil in a deep skillet until it reaches about 340°F (170°C). Using a spoon, scoop portions of the batter and carefully drop them into the hot oil, frying a few at a time for about 2-3 minutes per side, until golden and crispy. Turn the fritters gently to ensure even cooking and maintain a consistent oil temperature to prevent the fritters from absorbing too much oil. The sizzling sound and the golden color are indicators that the fritters are perfectly cooked.

4. **Cooling and Serving:** Drain the fritters on paper towels to remove excess oil, then place them on a wire rack to maintain their crispness. Serve them warm, garnished with a drizzle of honey to enhance the natural sweetness of the figs and a sprinkle of ground cinnamon. These fritters are perfect as a rustic dessert, simple yet rich with the flavors of autumn. The combination of the crunchy exterior and the soft, flavorful interior makes them an irresistible treat.

5. **Variations and Suggestions:**
   - **Spice Variations:** For a more complex flavor, you can add a pinch of nutmeg or ginger to the batter, enriching the aromatic profile of the fritters. These spices add warmth and depth, making the fritters even more comforting during the cooler months.
   - **Fresh Fig Option:** If you have fresh figs available, you can use them instead of dried figs, but be sure to reduce the amount of milk slightly to balance the additional moisture. Fresh figs add a different texture and a burst of juiciness, creating a delightful variation.
   - **Pairings:** These fritters pair wonderfully with a glass of sweet wine, such as Moscato, or with an herbal infusion to enhance the flavors of the dried fruit and spices. The sweetness of the wine or the aromatic notes of the herbal tea complements the rich, spiced flavor of the fritters, making them a perfect choice for a cozy autumn evening.

Conclusion: Rediscovering Medieval Flavors in Modern Times

Through this journey into medieval cuisine, we have explored the unique flavors, textures, and techniques that defined an era where food was not just nourishment, but an essential part of culture and society. Medieval cooking was an intricate blend of necessity, creativity, and cultural expression, deeply intertwined with the traditions, values, and beliefs of the time. The recipes presented here, along with their reinterpretations, invite us to reconnect with a time when cooking was an art influenced by seasonality, resourcefulness, and a profound respect for ingredients, revealing a world where every dish told a story.

The medieval kitchen was a place of ingenuity and resilience. With limited tools and a deep reliance on the natural world, cooks of the Middle Ages found ways to make flavors shine, transforming humble ingredients into dishes that could impress at both noble banquets and modest peasant tables. This creativity was fueled by an intimate knowledge of ingredients, as well as a drive to make the most of what was available in each season. This cookbook has sought to bridge the gap between those ancient practices and our modern kitchen, demonstrating that medieval cooking's creativity and adaptability still offer valuable lessons today. The techniques and methods developed back then—such as the use of herbs for seasoning, preserving food through drying or pickling, and creating elaborate dishes with minimal resources—remain relevant and inspiring for today's culinary enthusiasts.

In adapting these recipes for the present day, we aimed to retain the essence of medieval flavors while making them accessible to modern cooks. Ingredients that were once exotic, like saffron, cinnamon, and almond milk, are now within easy reach, allowing us to replicate the luxurious elements of medieval feasts. In medieval times, these ingredients were rare and expensive due to long trade routes and limited availability, making them symbols of wealth and prestige. The allure of these ingredients lay not only in their flavors but also in the stories they carried—saffron from distant lands, cinnamon as a mark of opulence, and almond milk as a versatile, dairy-free alternative for days of fasting. Meanwhile, practical substitutions and modern techniques have made it possible to enjoy these dishes without the challenges faced by our ancestors, ensuring that even those with a busy schedule can still experience the richness of these flavors.

This culinary exploration is not only about savoring the unique flavors and textures of medieval cuisine but also about preserving a cultural heritage that speaks of resilience, creativity, and the human spirit. By reinterpreting these dishes, we keep alive the traditions that shaped our history, while also celebrating the diversity and richness of flavors that medieval Europe brought to the world. The kitchen of the Middle Ages was a melting pot of influences—Arabic, Roman, and local European traditions all contributed to the evolving food culture. This diversity is reflected in the recipes we have shared, offering a glimpse into the confluence of cultures that helped shape the culinary landscape of Europe.

We hope this book has inspired you to experiment, to bring a piece of the past into your kitchen, and to share these timeless flavors with others. Cooking is, at its core, an act of sharing—a way to bring people together, to tell stories, and to connect across time and space. Whether you are hosting a medieval-themed dinner or exploring the culinary history of your region, these recipes provide a meaningful way to connect with the past. They allow you to savor timeless flavors in the present, creating a bridge that links the lives of those who lived centuries ago to our own experiences today. By preparing these dishes, you are not just cooking—you are becoming part of a lineage of cooks who have cherished the power of food to comfort, to nourish, and to delight.

Happy cooking—and may your kitchen be filled with the aromas and joys of the past, reimagined for today. May the stories and traditions of medieval cuisine inspire you to explore new flavors, to be resourceful with your ingredients, and to celebrate the enduring human connection that food brings. Let these recipes be a reminder that even in our fast-paced modern world, there is immense value in slowing down, in savoring each step of the cooking process, and in appreciating the rich heritage that each ingredient carries.

Conversion Tables

Volume Equivalents (Liquid)

US Standard	US Standard (ounces)	Metric (approximate)
2 tablespoons	1 fl. oz.	30 mL
¼ cup	2 fl. oz.	60 mL
½ cup	4 fl. oz.	120 mL
1 cup	8 fl. oz.	240 mL
1½ cups	12 fl. oz.	355 mL
2 cups or 1 pint	16 fl. oz.	475 mL
4 cups or 1 quart	32 fl. oz.	1 L
1 gallon	128 fl. oz.	4 L

Volume Equivalents (Dry)

US Standard	Metric (approximate)
⅛ teaspoon	0.5 mL
¼ teaspoon	1 mL
½ teaspoon	2 mL
¾ teaspoon	4 mL
1 teaspoon	5 mL
1 tablespoon	15 mL
¼ cup	59 mL
⅓ cup	79 mL
½ cup	118 mL
⅔ cup	156 mL
¾ cup	177 mL
1 cup	235 mL
2 cups or 1 pint	475 mL
3 cups	700 mL
4 cups or 1 quart	1 L

Oven Temperatures

Fahrenheit (F)	Celsius (C) (approximate)
250°F	120°C
300°F	150°C
325°F	165°C
350°F	180°C
375°F	190°C
400°F	200°C
425°F	220°C
450°F	230°C

Weight Equivalents

US Standard	Metric (approximate)
1 tablespoon	15 g
½ ounce	15 g
1 ounce	30 g
2 ounces	60 g
4 ounces	115 g
8 ounces	225 g
12 ounces	340 g
16 ounces or 1 pound	455 g

Made in the USA
Monee, IL
21 December 2024

75006349R00069